White Awareness

ANTI-RACISM TRAINING

By Judith H. Katz

University of Oklahoma Press : Norman and London

Library of Congress Cataloging-in-Publication Data

Katz, Judith H., 1950–
　White awareness.

Bibliography: p. 201
　Includes index.
　1. Racism.　2. Race discrimination—Psychological aspects.
3. Caucasian race.　4. Group relations training.　5. Race awareness.　6. Racism.—United States.　I. Title.
HT1523.K37　　　301.45'1'042　　　77–18610
ISBN: 0–8061–1466–5

7　8　9　10　11　12　13　14　15　16　17　18　19　20　21

Preface

A Personal Note

As I reflect on the development of this book, I recall the many hours, days, months, and years that have gone into putting it together, both in me and on paper. It grew out of my personal and professional struggle to understand and come to grips with racism.

The issue of racism is one of very deep concern to me. Becoming aware of racism and owning my whiteness has been a long process. It is a process that I have often fought and rejected inside myself. It is a process that has been marked by introspection, confrontation, anger, frustration, confusion, and guilt on the one hand and the joy of discovering another level in me and finding a new sense of personal freedom on the other.

The roots of this process—and this book—go back to early childhood. My parents, who are Jewish, were forced to leave Germany during World War II. They settled in New York City, and I grew up there. Their concerns about equality and fairness they often discussed and shared with me as a young child. Their own experiences with discrimination and the impact of it on their lives became evident to me as I grew up and were an important foundation for my later exploration of racism.

It was not, however, until my college years in the late 1960s that racism made a personal impact on my life. I became involved with the human relations movement and sensitivity training. In this forum I became introspective and began to examine some of my values and behaviors. My interaction with minority students and professors helped me begin to see other perspectives and acknowledge that racism does indeed exist.

The real "unfreezing point" in my perspective came as a result of a six-day residential seminar held in 1970. The participant population was 85 percent Puerto Rican and Black and 15 percent White. For the first time in my life I found myself in a situation that was not White- or Jewish-dominated. I was immersed in a different culture. I was confronted both subtly and overtly with my whiteness, my assumptions, and my values. Being no longer the "norm," I felt the need to seek out the support of other White people—to eat, talk, socialize, and identify with them. I found myself feeling defensive about my whiteness and guilty and hurt because I was labeled the oppressor.

During the workshop sessions the issue of racism came to the fore. I wanted not to be seen as a racist, and I shared with the group my feelings of guilt, as well as my concern about racism. The reaction from the minority participants was some understanding of my concern; however, in their view my concern did not go far enough. My guilt did not bring about any change in their living with oppression, nor was it healthy for me. Essentially my guilt was a self-indulgent way to use up energy. The real issue was not whether I was concerned about combating racism but what I had done to combat it. What *action* had I taken? My not doing was a way of supporting and perpetuating racism. Inaction is action. I was strongly told, "Don't sit here telling us what you would like to do—do it! And make sure you take that action where it needs to be taken—to the White community, where the problem is."

It was in that experience that the importance of action became meaningful to me. The question, What have you done? has been the motivating force in my search to uncover racism within myself and to combat racism actively. This training program is an attempt to answer the question and a partial response to the need to find a meaningful way to help create change in the White community.

The program offered in this book developed out of my work with sensitivity-training groups. After participating in many Black-White T-groups, I began to realize that all too often minorities were being put on the hot seat to discuss their experiences with oppression. Whites would often attempt to refute the reality of those experiences or would feel guilty about being White. Often White people left the experience seeing a particular Black person as "different" from other Blacks, confirming their initial attitudes or views or feeling a great deal of anxiety and guilt about being White. Blacks often left feeling angry or hopeless. These dynamics, coupled with my awareness of the need for action in the White community, led me to think about White-on-White groups as a way to address racism in White people. In 1972, I began facilitating White-on-White groups in Amherst, Massachusetts. Over the succeeding years this process crystallized into a systematic conceptual and experiential format.

to break
oppressor
role

This book is, therefore, designed for White people. It is a means to help us break out of the oppressor role and take a step toward being more fully human. We have learned from the Feminist Movement that men as well as women are adversely affected by oppressive sex roles. Similarly, Whites too suffer from racism. It is my hope that this training program will help White people not only deal with racist ideologies to which we have been conditioned but also come to terms with our guilt, our need to feel superior, our denial of our racism, and our whiteness. This program provides a method to help Whites liberate themselves from the oppressiveness of racism in their lives.

Third
vs
First
Hierarchy

One of the problems in dealing with racism is that of finding appropriate terminology to identify groups. I have used the terms "Third World" and "minorities" to describe people of color in the United States. They include Asian-Americans, Blacks, Chicanos, Native Americans, and Puerto Ricans. I am aware that some groups may respond negatively to these terms. "Third World" can be interpreted as yet another form of racism developed by ethnocentrism (First World being Western capitalist countries, including the United States), and "minorities" can be interpreted as a denial of the fact that in the world population people of color are a majority. It is my hope that the reader will take into account the imperfection of our language and recognize that these terms are here used to describe and not to oppress people of color in the United States.

Many of the exercises and discussions in this book focus on Black-White relations. This is not to imply that other peoples of color in the United States do not experience the oppression of racism. I have focused on Black-White relations as one pervasive example. It would be useful to discuss the effects of racism on other minority groups. The facilitator should be aware of both the similarities of the effects of racism on all these minority groups and the unique ramifications of oppression on each group.

Although this book is in a "final" form, I do not assume that the search has ended. Each time I return to the premises upon which the book is based, I find new insight, new direction, new perspectives from which to view myself. May it serve you as a starting place or as a means to continue your journey.

It is my goal that we may ultimately find comfort in our move toward liberation, no matter how painful the self-probing may be. As Whites we must deal with our racism so that all people may be

vii

free. It is through this process of self-examination, change, and action that we will someday liberate ourselves and our society.

To cite all those persons who have played some part either directly or indirectly in the preparation of this book could be a volume in itself. I would like to thank the colleagues and friends who put their time and faith both in my work and in me. Their support, their encouragement, their listening and critical comments have helped this book grow and develop.

I am deeply grateful to my friend and colleague Al Ivey. Al's skills, knowledge, and drive for achievement have been important role models for me. Through his guidance, concerns for excellence, perfection, and scholarship have become parts of me. Special thanks go to Bobby Daniels, a humanist who lives by his convictions. He has taught me how to relate in the world in nonoppressive ways. I am grateful to Lee Bolman, whose honesty and commitment to consistency raised important theoretical and pragmatic questions about the implications of my approach. Our conversations—and frequent battles—in retrospect were an important source of learning for me.

Craig Washington, Bailey Jackson, Nancy Meneely, Thea Servente, and Norma Jean Anderson, all friends at the University of Massachusetts, have added richness to my life both personally and professionally.

Appreciation for their support, insights, and time go to Andrea Wilson, Kris Libbee, Jan Bentz, Richard Davis, and George Henderson. In their own ways they have provided me with the courage to continue this project during a very trying time.

Thanks are due Carol Cox, Eve Shank, and Larry Bishop, who worked painstakingly in typing and retyping the manuscript.

Finally, my gratitude goes to my parents, who have not always understood my endeavors but still have given their never-ending love. Their ability to stand by and cheer me on even when they disagree is greatly appreciated.

JUDITH H. KATZ

Norman, Oklahoma

Contents

		Page
Preface	A Personal Note	v
Part I	Introduction	1
Chapter 1	Racism and Human Relations Training	3
Chapter 2	Racism as a White Problem: Theoretical Perspectives and Overview	7
Chapter 3	How to Use This Program	22
Part II	The Training Program	31
Stage 1	Racism: Definitions and Inconsistencies	32
	Readings	186
	Resources	197
Stage 2	Confronting the Reality of Racism	53
	Readings	188
	Resources	197
Stage 3	Dealing with Feelings	93
	Readings	190
	Resources	197
Stage 4	Cultural Differences: Exploring Cultural Racism	109
	Readings	191
	Resources	197
Stage 5	The Meaning of Whiteness: Individual Racism	135
	Readings	193
	Resources	197

Stage 6   Developing Action Strategies   167
          Readings   195
          Resources   197

Appendix   Readings and Resources   185
           Readings   185
           Resources (Suppliers)   197

Bibliography   201

Index   207

PART ONE Introduction

CHAPTER 1

Racism and Human Relations Training

The importance of human relations training has been increasingly recognized over the past few decades. As such training has become more widespread, people have begun to deal with issues that before were rarely addressed in open and systematic ways. People are examining questions about such issues as identity, exploration of relationships, and sexuality and sex roles.

Human relations training means different things to different people. To some, it focuses on understanding oneself with the goals of identifying one's individuality and moving toward self-actualization. To others, improving relationships with friends, family, loved ones, and co-workers is of major concern. To many, human relations training implies improving relationships in organizations to create a more productive and effective work environment. To still others, it is a means of diagnosing and eliminating such forms of oppression as racism, sexism, and agism in an effort to make the world a better place in which to live.

Out of these concerns have come many programs. Counseling centers offer developmental counseling in such areas as interpersonal relations, life planning, sex roles, divorce, and death. Schools are including humanistic and psychological education in their curricula in an effort to teach students the affective as well as cognitive skills necessary for productive living. Businesses are offering organization development to focus on the processes that are carried out in an organization in addition to the making of the product.

All these programs are useful ways to make environments more humane for the individuals who function in them. Several problems emerge from these approaches, however. In an effort to be more humane the tendency is often to emphasize similarities in people and to overlook or dismiss their differences. Many programs in education, counseling, organizations, and human relations training concentrate solely on the individual, paying little attention to the culture and environment from which the individual comes. It is often simplistic to ignore or try to transcend some of the real differences between individuals and between groups of people. We cannot over-

3

look who and what we are as people. We cannot dismiss the fact that being a woman or a man and being a Black, an Asian-American, a Chicano, a Native American, or a Caucasian are important aspects of our lives. Our sexual and racial essences have an enormous influence on our perspectives and experiences. Each of us must acknowledge and explore these parts of ourselves to discover our unique identities. In fact, Roberts (1975) states that we are not a complete people until we deal with the seven significant areas of which we are comprised: personal, sexual, family, ethnic or racial, social class, provincial, and cultural.

The implications of coming to terms with the socialization processes of sex role and sexuality have become increasingly evident as the Women's Movement has grown. So too racial identity deeply influences how we see and interact in the world. This concept has long been acknowledged in relation to minorities. Much research has been done on the effects of racism on the self-concept and perspective of minorities. Little research, however, has been done on the effects of racism on Whites. In fact, it seems fair to say that, because the White race has been considered the norm in United States culture, racism has simply been overlooked as an issue in the White community. The attitude seems to be that if minorities are not physically present the problem of racism does not exist. Whites easily forget—indeed are seldom aware—that they too are part of a group and are subject to ethnocentrism and a unique collective group experience.

The reality is: racism exists. It has been a part of the American way of life since the first Whites landed on the continent. Although the United States prides itself on its ideologies about human rights and particularly on its philosophies of freedom and equality, the bleak reality is that, both historically and presently, this country is based on and operates under a doctrine of White racism. It can be seen historically in White people's interactions with Native Americans, in the development of the doctrine of manifest destiny, in the establishment of Indian reservations, in the capture and enslavement of Africans, in the wartime internment of Japanese-Americans, and presently in the pervasive attitude of most White Americans that Third World Americans must "fight" for their rights—the same rights that White Americans enjoy from birth. Racism is manifested not only in the minority ghettos of the cities but equally in the White ghettos of the suburbs, in the South, and in the North. Racism es-

4

capes no one. It is a part of us all and has deeply infiltrated the lives and psyches of both the oppressed and the oppressors.

The task that confronts educators, counselors, facilitators, and change agents is developing a way of identifying the issues of racism as they exist in the *White* community and helping *White* people grow and learn about themselves as Whites in this society. How can we help White people come out from behind the myths that have sheltered them for so long and begin focusing on the difficult realities and discrepancies that are present in American society?

This training program is an attempt to answer that question. It is designed to be used primarily by counselors, teachers, educators, change agents, and facilitators who are concerned about helping individuals examine their attitudes and behaviors as Whites and the implications of their own racism in order to become more fully human. The program has been adapted and used in school systems with teachers, counselors, and administrators; as part of Affirmative Action Programs with managers; in university communities with students, faculties, and administrators. The program has also served as the foundation for a paraprofessional program for counselors who facilitate their own racial awareness programs in dormitories. One major key to the program is its flexibility and adaptability to many different settings.

The program is one of liberation that is designed to go beyond rhetoric by presenting a systematic means of facilitating change in White people's racist attitudes and behaviors. The real test of the program is whether or not it works. Does it produce change in the attitudes and behaviors of White people? Do they become anti-racist? The results of research on the program's effectiveness indicate that attitudes and behaviors do change significantly in a positive direction after completion of the workshop. A recent follow-up study showed that changes in attitudes and behaviors had been maintained (Katz and Ivey, 1977). Participants had become actively engaged in developing new curricula for schools, eliminating racism from their language, taking active roles in the governance of their organizations, examining criteria for hiring, facilitating workshops on racial awareness, and educating friends, families, and co-workers. These significant behaviors are evidence that racism can be effectively countered in positive, active directions.

Before turning to the program itself, the facilitator using this handbook should be aware of some of the basic premises on which it is based. Chapter 2 offers a theoretical statement and rationale of racism as a White problem, explores some of the effects of racism on White people, examines the need for change in White people's lives, and looks at various programs that have been developed to combat racism. The need for a systematic, step-by-step training program is established, and some of the implications for research on racism awareness training are examined.

Chapter 3 presents an overview of the training program, together with suggestions on adapting it for different settings, alternative designs, and instructions for the facilitator.

Each stage of the six-stage program is presented in Part II. Specific exercises and experiences are provided to facilitate learning on both cognitive and affective levels. A list of resources, including reading lists; films, tapes, records, and other workshop materials; and suppliers, is given in the Appendix.

CHAPTER 2

Racism as a White Problem: Theoretical Perspectives and Overview

Introduction

Over the years attention and concern have been given to the effect of racism on the quality of life of all Americans. Over seventy years ago W. E. B. Du Bois (1903) examined the effects of racism on Blacks and Whites. Almost thirty-five years ago Swedish sociologist Gunnar Myrdal (1944) called racism "an American Dilemma." Calls for Black, Red, Yellow, and Brown Power were echoing in the 1960s. In 1968 the Kerner Commission concluded that racism is a White problem. In recent years Francis Cress Welsing (1972) has explored White superiority as a defense mechanism developed in response to White people's numerical inferiority to people of color throughout the world. Such issues as Affirmative Action, busing, integration, and self-concept have been the focus of discussions of the effects of racism on American citizens. Writers, historians, researchers, and activists have shown racism to be a social, political, economic, and psychological force that has permeated the lives and perspectives of both the oppressed and the oppressors.

Even with all of this attention to the issue, however, it appears that little change is occurring. The ghettos continue to grow; integration and busing are volatile issues not only in the South but in the North as well; the ranks of the Ku Klux Klan and the John Birch Society continue to expand; and Affirmative Action efforts are being met with cries of "reverse discrimination." Because of these conditions and the state of our society today, it is essential to focus on racism as it affects the oppressors—namely, White people. This chapter will seek to establish the nature of racism as a White problem, describe its effects on Whites both psychologically and intellectually, and discuss the processes that are necessary to bring about change in the attitudes and behaviors of Whites.

Despite all the writings in the field, little has been published on racism as it affects Whites. Few strategies or materials have been designed to raise the consciousness of White people, to help them identify racism in themselves and others, or to develop skills to facilitate change in the White community. Although there is a great deal

7

of rhetoric about the need for change and the destructiveness of racism, the strategies developed to alleviate the problem are often merely new training programs for minorities. The victim, not the victimizer, once again becomes the target for change. The symptoms are attacked instead of the cause. For example, even in multicultural education programs that are attempting to break down rigid cultural barriers, we find much emphasis on appreciation of differences but little implementation of these programs and concepts in all-White areas, where the cultural isolation may be the greatest. Until the real perpetuators of racism are confronted and educated, little will change. Whites need to examine the discrepancies between American ideals and American reality. Until those discrepancies are uncovered, White Americans will continue to live a personal lie and maintain a false sense of their identity in the world. Some of the realities of racism and its insidious effects on Whites are discussed below.

Racism as a White Problem

To examine racism in America today, one must first explore its roots and development. White racism has a history of over 350 years (Bennett, 1966; Jordan, 1968; Kovel, 1970). The foundations of racism and the present-day racist system were established in western European and especially English ideology and language. According to Schwartz and Disch (1970):

> By the time the first English colonists had arrived in the New World they had already inherited a host of associations tied to the word "black" which became important as men put language to use in first defining and later justifying the status they desired of non-whites. [P. 6]

When the colonists arrived on this continent, these basically negative attitudes of Whites toward peoples of color went into the formulation of racist practices and policies (Lacy, 1972). This is evident in the account by Joyce (n. d.):

> From the time the first Native American "Indian" died at the hands of a European settler (if not before), the United States has held white supremacy as a dominant theme in its institutional and cultural life. The "New World" civilization ultimately de-

8

stroyed nearly one half of the "Indian" population (genocide by any criteria), defined in its basic political document the black person as three fifths of a man, and created a chattel slavery system more dehumanizing and destructive than any the world has ever known. [P. 1]

Such is the basis of racism in America. From the time of formalized slavery to the present Whites have oppressed Third World people through the perpetuation of racism at every level of life. It is present in our institutions, our culture, and our individual actions (Haley, 1967; Jones, 1972; Kerner Commission, 1968; Kovel, 1970; Schwartz and Disch, 1970; Terry, 1970; Yette, 1971).

It becomes evident from a review of current literature and events that racism is still a very serious and explosive issue in America today (Jones, 1972; Knowles and Prewitt, 1969; Kovel, 1970; Schwartz and Disch, 1970; Terry, 1970; Yette, 1971; Welsing, 1972). In a recent government study the Kerner Commission (1968) concluded that

what white Americans have never fully understood—but what the Negro can never forget—is that white society is deeply implicated in the ghetto. White institutions created it, white institutions maintain it and white society condones it. . . . White racism is essentially responsible for the explosive mixture which has been accumulating in our cities since the end of World War II. [P. 2]

The Kerner report specified what racism is and described how Whites support it. Whitney Young (1970) supported the Kerner Commission's findings:

Most Americans get awfully uptight about the charge of racism, since most people are not conscious of what racism really is. Racism is not a desire to wake up every morning and lynch a black man from a tall tree. It is not engaging in vulgar epithets. These kinds of people are just fools. It is the day to day indignities, the subtle humiliations, that are so devastating. Racism is the assumption of superiority of one group over another, with all the gross arrogance that goes along with it. Racism is a part of us.

9

The Kerner Commission has said that if you have been an observer you have been racist; if you have stood by idly, you are racist. [P. 730]

Joseph R. Barndt (1970) summarized the essence of racism in America:

If a man is seriously ill, and doctor after doctor incorrectly diagnoses the sickness and prescribes the wrong medicine, that is a tragedy. But if a doctor finally comes along and correctly identifies the illness and prescribes the proper medicine for a cure, then it is time for a celebration.

The name of the illness is "white racism!"—a hard fact to accept, and an even harder fact to change. But at least it is out in the open. [P. 15]

In summary, racism is a White problem in that its development and perpetuation rest with White people. Whites created racism through the establishment of policies and practices that serve to their advantage and benefit and continue to oppress all minorities in the United States. Racism is perpetuated by Whites through their conscious and/or unconscious support of a culture and institutions that are founded on racist policies and practices. The racial prejudice of White people coupled with the economic, political, and social power to enforce discriminatory practices on every level of life—cultural, institutional, and individual—is the gestalt of White racism. Therefore, the "race problem" in America is essentially a *White* problem in that it is Whites who developed it, perpetuate it, and have the power to resolve it.

Effects of Racism on White People

Most of the studies of racism focus on the oppressed—that is, the minorities. It is clear from research and observation that White racism is and has been responsible for the physiological, sociological, and psychological genocide of Third World people (Brown, 1970; Fanon, 1968; Yette, 1971; Lacy, 1972; Grier and Cobbs, 1968; Haley, 1967). Given that the root of the problem rests in the White community, it seems almost ironic that so much of the research focuses on the oppressed instead of the oppressors. Racism has taken

10

its toll on White people as well. It has been hypothesized that, in a somewhat different way, racism is just as dehumanizing for Whites as it is for minorities (Cobbs, 1972; Kovel, 1970; Du Bois, 1903). Berry pointed this out in his book *The Hidden Wound* (1970):

> If white people have suffered less obviously from racism than black people, they have nevertheless suffered greatly; the cost has been greater perhaps than we yet know. If the white man has inflicted the wound of racism upon black men, the cost has been that he would receive the mirror image of that wound into himself. [P. 2]

Du Bois (1920) eloquently described the dehumanizing effect of racism on Whites:

> Unfortunate? Unfortunate. But where is the misfortune? Mine? Am I, in my blackness, the sole sufferer? I suffer. And yet, somehow, above the suffering, above the shackled anger that beats the bars, above the hurt that crazes there surges in me a vast pity— pity for a people imprisoned and enthralled, hampered and made miserable for such a cause, for such a phantasy! [Pp. 33–34]

Other authors have begun to investigate in some depth the effects of racism on Whites. It appears clear that it has a very serious psychological effect (Beck, 1973; Berry, 1970; Citron, 1969; Casselli, 1971; Jones, 1972). The United States Commission on Mental Health (1965) declared:

> ... the racist attitude of Americans which causes and perpetuates tension is patently a most compelling health hazard. Its destructive effects severely cripple the growth and development of millions of our citizens young and old alike.

Several authors have probed the disease more deeply. Wendell Berry (1970), a White, describes racism as a disease with which he has been afflicted from birth and from which, though he is trying to overcome it, he suffers every day.

Racism has been diagnosed as a form of schizophrenia in that there is a large gap between what Whites believe and what they actually practice, which causes them to live in a state of psychological stress

(Allen, 1971; Bidol, 1971). Myrdal, in his study of the "race problem" in America (1944), concluded that racism underlay every facet
of life in the United States—political, economic, and social. At the
bottom of the problem, however, he found the White citizens' moral
dilemma:

> ... the deep cultural and psychological conflict among the Amer-
> ican people of American ideals of equality, freedom, God-given
> dignity of the individual, inalienable rights on the one hand,
> against practices of discrimination, humiliation, insult, denial
> of opportunity to Negroes and others in a racist society on the
> other. [P. lxxi]

Myrdal was telling us that the level of interaction and conceptualiza-
tion is based on a serious discrepancy between attitude and action,
between thought and deed. The White American citizen talks about
equality and says that she or he believes in it. Yet alongside this
profession is the truth of oppression and denial of selfhood to citizens of other colors (Katz and Ivey, 1977).

Other authors offer theories that see racism as a disease. Thomas
and Sillen (1972) find that racism is deeply rooted in personality.
Comer (1972), a Black psychiatrist, elaborates on this point in his
analysis of racism. He describes it as a "low level defense and adjustment mechanism similar to the manner in which individuals utilize
psyche defenses and adjustment mechanisms to deal with anxiety"
(p. 311). Delaney (1972) further identifies the disease by breaking
down racism into elements that include acting out, denial of reality,
projection, transference of blame, disassociation, and justification.
All these elements are basic characteristics of destructive behavior.
Psychologist Kenneth Clark (1963) noted that, in "normal forms of
expressions of prejudice among average Americans, one observes
certain types of reactions which, if demonstrated with other members
of an individual's own race, would be considered symptoms of emotional disturbance" (p. 77). All these analyses clearly indicate that
racism is a critical and pervasive form of mental illness.

It is also crucial to explore how the disease is manifested in observ-
able traits and ideologies. One way is through the delusion of White
superiority (Bidol, 1971; Citron, 1969; Kovel, 1970; Brown, 1972;
Welsing, 1972; Jordan, 1968). Racism and ethnocentric ideologies
envelop White people so that they are unable to experience themselves

12

and their culture *as it is*. Du Bois (1920), in his essay "The Souls of White Folk," looked at how the attitude of superiority is displayed in Whites. Du Bois saw it as an arrogance coupled with a disdain for everyone and everything non-White. That has been perpetuated through omission and emphasis, leading to a belief that everything great that was ever done in the world was the work of Whites.

The superior attitude "White is right" often leaves Whites confused about their identity (Bidol, 1971). Beck (1973) stated that "the confusion of the meaning of whiteness leads many Whites to think that all America is white." (p. 23). Because United States culture is centered around White norms, White people rarely have to come to terms with that part of their identity. Ask a White person his or her race, and you may get the response "Italian," "Jewish," "Irish," "English," and so on. *White people do not see themselves as White.* This is a way of denying responsibility for perpetuating the racist system and being part of the problem. By seeing oneself solely as an individual, one can disown one's racism. Lack of understanding of self owing to a poor sense of identity causes Whites to develop a negative attitude toward minorities on both a conscious and a subconscious level (Allen, 1971; Quarles, 1964; Schwartz and Disch, 1970).

Some of the literature focuses on the development of racist attitudes in children. Goodman's study (1964) indicated that children are infected with racism as early as age four. She elicited concepts and feelings on race from White four-year-olds and concluded from their remarks and the tone of the statements that by that age they had already internalized feelings of superiority. Singh and Yancey (1974) found negative racial attitudes among first-grade White children. Morland (1962) noted that the preference for being White and the negative attitude of White children toward Blacks were based not necessarily upon direct negative contact with Blacks but rather upon subtle communication from parents, teachers, the media, and so on. Other studies have further indicated a strong preference by very young White children for the color white and a negative connotation for the color black. This is transferred to Black people (Singh and Yancey, 1974; Greenwald and Oppenheim, 1968; Robinson and Spaights, 1969). Citron (1969) best sums up the over-all effects of racism on the White child:

White-centeredness is not the reality of his world, but he is under the illusion that it is. It is thus impossible for him to deal accu-

13

rately or adequately with the universe of human and social relationships. . . . He also learns salience, that is, what portions of his environment are important to him, and to which he must react. He learns in his white world the importance of reacting in a certain way to skin color. . . . Children who develop this pattern learn dependence on a psychological and moral crutch which inhibits and deforms the growth of a healthy and responsible personality. . . . Children who develop in this way are robbed of opportunities for emotional and intellectual growth, stunted in basic development of the self so that they cannot experience or accept humanity. This is a personality outcome in which it is quite possible to build into children a great feeling and compassion for animals and an unconscious fear and rejection of differing human beings. Such persons are by no means prepared to live and move with either appreciation or effectiveness in today's world. [Pp. 14–16]

From these studies it becomes sadly evident that the psychological disorder racism is deeply imbedded in White people from a very early age on both a conscious and an unconscious level. The disease has locked them in a psychological prison that victimizes and oppresses them every day of their lives (Barndt, 1970).

Racism has also been found to cripple White people intellectually (Beck, 1973; Citron, 1969; Daniels, 1974). In their study of institutional racism in America, Knowles and Prewitt (1969) indicated that White children are miseducated. United States history and foreign affairs are distorted through superficial and inconsistent treatment of minority Americans. Racial issues are rarely dealt with realistically or recorded accurately. Over all, texts and information serve to re-emphasize White Americans and omit other Americans' contributions to society. White people, as well as Third World people, have been miseducated about their true historical roots (Daniels, 1973). James Weldon Johnson (1960), equating White with Anglo-Saxon, discussed this issue:

Can you name a single one of the great fundamental and intellectual achievements which have raised man in the scale of civilization that may be credited to the Anglo-Saxon? The art of letters, of poetry, of music, of sculpture, of painting, of the drama, of architecture; the science of mathematics, of astronomy, of philosophy, of logic, of physics, of chemistry, the use of metals, and the principles of mechanics, were all invented or discovered by darker and what we now call inferior races and nations. . . . Do you know that the only original contribution to civilization we can claim is what we have done in steam and electricity and in making implements of war more deadly? And there we worked largely on principles we did not discover. Why, we didn't even originate the religion we use. . . . If the Anglo-Saxon is the source of everything good and great in the human race from the beginning, why wasn't the German forest the birthplace of civilization, rather than the valley of the Nile? [Pp. 162–63]

Citron (1969) summarizes the effects of racism on Whites:

The white ghetto creates exactly the kinds of beings who act as if they are on the other side of a thick pane of glass, not only from Negroes, but from the real world. They are blandly unconcerned, unaware, operating in an aura of assumed rightness and unconscious superiority.

The white-centered, provincial, insulated, imperialistic mentality of white ghettoization acts as blinders over the eyes of children, and cotton in their ears, imprisoning the minds, shackling the spirits, crippling the personality. [P. 12]

It is clear that racism has severely hindered White people's psychological and intellectual development. In psychological terms racism has deluded Whites into a false sense of superiority that has left them in a pathological and schizophrenic state. In intellectual terms racism has resulted in miseducation about the realities of history, the contributions of Third World people, and the role of White people in present-day culture. The intellectual perspective and growth potential of Whites has been severely limited owing to racism.

Mechanisms for Change

A number of authors, agreeing that action to deal with racism is imperative, have discussed the need for strategies to combat it. The strategies that seem to be the most widely supported by Third World people and by aware Whites are those that place emphasis on White involvement within their own communities (Bennett, 1966; Knowles and Prewitt, 1969; Cleaver, 1968; Welsing, 1974; Edler, 1974;

Coppard and Steinwachs, 1970). Malcolm X (Breitman, 1970) clearly supported such action:

> Whites who are sincere should organize themselves and figure out some strategies to break down the prejudice that exists in white communities. This is where they can function more intelligently and more effectively, in the white community itself, and this has never been done. [P. 164]

Stokely Carmichael (Carmichael and Hamilton, 1967) also stressed this approach: "If the white man wants to help he can go home and free his own people."
Robert Terry (1970), a White, elaborated on this point:

> What is at stake for white America today is not what black people want and do but what white people stand for and do. The racial problem is not a "black problem," it is a "white problem." If there are any racial ambiguities, conflicts, and contradictions in black America, it is only because these factors are deeper and more far reaching in white America. The time has come to attack the causes of racial crisis, not the victims. [P. 15]

The need for reeducation of White people is stressed in a statement by the United States Commission on Civil Rights (1970): "The principal task of those white Americans combating racism lies with the white community, rather than within the non-white communities" (p. 39).

In the fields of human relations and education a number of techniques have been developed to deal with racism. One mechanism designed to lessen racial and ethnic tensions is the interracial encounter group (Kranz, 1972; Walker and Hamilton, 1973; Cobbs, 1972; Wilkinson, 1973). This process grew out of sensitivity-training techniques (Marrow, 1967) and developed into a more structured, confrontive group (Winter, 1971). The technique deals with the participants' affective level of consciousness. The basic premise of the encounter-group process is that interracial communications will improve and subsequently lead to positive action (Walker and Hamilton, 1973).

Rubin's work with T-groups indicated that such groups can lessen racial prejudice. At the end of a T-group made up of eight Whites

16

and two Blacks, Rubin found a significant decrease in racial prejudice (Rubin, 1967). The encounter group of Walker and Hamilton (1973), consisting of six Blacks, four Chicanos, and four Whites, also appeared to result in a reduction of interracial tensions. A similar model was developed to increase teachers' capacity to relate to others regardless of race (Golden, 1970). Still another interracial confrontation group, this one in a junior college, produced some positive results: Both Black and White participants felt better about each other (Kranz, 1972).

Although it appears from these findings that the interracial encounter group is a useful tool for changing attitudes, one must look a bit deeper at the data presented. One problem that arises with interracial group experiences is that the functioning of the groups may itself be racist. Kranz (1972), describing his racial confrontation group, opens by saying:

> Historically, whites have exhorted non-whites to make changes so that they would be acceptable as full fledged Americans. However, events in the U.S. have shown the dishonesty and tragedy of this emphasis. *Therefore, a major focus of each group was to help whites* see that they must learn and change within themselves if further violence is to be avoided. [P. 70, italics added]

Ironically, the same condition exists in all similar interracial group processes; that is, the responsibility to facilitate change remains on minority-group members. Minorities are placed in the position of teaching White people, being given the same responsibility that Kranz himself notes they have historically been given. Thus the interracial encounter group may often serve as simply another form of exploitation of minorities for White people's purposes. The benefit seems to be greater for Whites than for Third World people. This is contrary to the premise that Whites must learn to help themselves (Terry, 1970; Bidol, 1971; Edler, 1974).

Other techniques, designed mainly for educational settings, have been developed to produce changes in racist attitudes through a cognitive approach. One is the simulation game. Through the administration of pre and post attitude surveys, DeKock (1969) concluded that a simulation game dealing with racism did produce attitude change. Other cognitive approaches have included the teaching of race-relations history (Synnestvedt, 1970). The course focused on

17

the realities of racism in America to counteract the miseducation that the system perpetuates. Bidol and Weber (1970) developed a social-studies curriculum for secondary schools that includes activities designed to give students a more realistic historical view of racism in America. John M. Hunter (1972) described a package of courses examining the societal, political, and economic bases of racism.

One drawback to the cognitive approach is that there are very few data on the success of the mechanisms in changing racist attitudes and behaviors. Given the nature of the miseducation, the cognitive approach appears to be greatly needed. Malcolm X (Breitman, 1970) supported this position:

> If the entire American population were properly educated—by properly educated, I mean given the true picture of the history and contributions of the black man—I think many whites would be less racist in their feelings. They would have more respect for the black man as a human being. Knowing what the black man's contributions to science and civilization have been in the past, the white man's feelings of superiority would be at least partially negated. . . . So it takes education to eliminate it. And just because you have colleges and universities doesn't mean you have education. The colleges and universities in the American educational system are skillfully used to miseducate. [Pp. 160–61]

Although this approach appears to be an important one in changing White people's racist attitudes and potentially in affecting behavior, it falls short in that it does not deal with the psychological and affective sides of those attitudes.

A significant approach to combating racism that has recently emerged in education is the development of multicultural curricula (Gay, 1973; Banks, 1975). These programs are designed to help students understand and appreciate cultural differences. Multicultural curricula attempt to introduce children (and their teachers) to the concept that indeed there is no one model American (American Association of Colleges for Teacher Education, 1972). The overarching goal of these programs is to bring educational systems and subsequently the nation into line with the ideals of a pluralistic society. That is precisely the direction that is needed. At present, however, there are several shortcomings in multicultural education. One is that these programs tend to be implemented only in racially

18

mixed schools. They fail to reach White children isolated in suburban or rural areas who also need to develop an awareness and understanding of people who are culturally different from themselves.

A second shortcoming is that these programs often focus on minority cultures without a complementary focus on White culture. It is assumed that only White history is being taught in the schools and that therefore there is no need to give it more attention. Although this assumption is partly correct, in that White history has been taught as "American" history, the effect on White and minority children is to maintain a miseducated view of being White. What is needed is reeducation and a realistic focus on the role that White people have played in shaping United States history. This crucial step is often overlooked.

Finally, in multicultural education programs there is much discussion of the need for minority students to develop a positive sense of identity—the assumption being that Whites already have that positive sense of self. But Whites also need to identify themselves as White and feel good about it. This does not minimize the need of the minority community but rather acknowledges faulty assumptions that have been made about Whites for too long.

One technique designed to address the issue of being White is the White-on-White training group. Expanding on the belief that White people must work within the White community (Cleaver, 1968; Terry, 1970; Steinberg, n. d.), these groups were developed so that Whites could explore their racism without exploiting minorities (Elder, 1974; Moore, 1973; Bidol, 1971). Some of the White-on-White experiences focus on affective issues (Moore, 1973), while others are structured to deal with cognitive issues (Bidol, 1971; Timmel, n. d.). The purpose of these groups is to create a positive change in attitudes and move White people to take action to combat racism (Terry, 1970).

Moore (1973) has shown that this technique is successful. Moore facilitated a number of White-on-White workshops and found a positive change in White teachers' racial attitudes. In this area there is a great need for further development of resources, specifically, a developmental process to assure positive change in both attitudes and behaviors. The program of this book grew out of that need.

It is important to look at other training techniques to learn about the methods that are being employed, even in areas that are not directly related to combating racism. In the fields of human relations, psy-

19

chology, education, and counseling it appears that systematic training is being used because it has been extremely successful in achieving behavior change. Authier, Gustafson, Guerney, and Kasdorf (1975) extensively reviewed the literature to identify trends in psychotherapy. They concluded that the field is moving from a therapeutic model toward a more educational role for the psychotherapist and is utilizing systematic training as the process by which to meet desired behavior change. The shifts from psychotherapist and patient to psychoteacher and student roles provide a broader outlook for the counselor-client relationship. This approach, developed from learning theory, has been expanded into the view of the help a client receives as a learning process. Psychotherapy, the authors note, has begun to focus more on prevention of psychosocial problems and less on remediation. This long-range focus has produced a shift in role from that of therapist to that of educator. Ivey (1976) elaborated on the concept of counselor as teacher. Counseling centers throughout the country are implementing systematic programs in an effort to address developmental and preventive needs of clients in addition to remedial treatment (Katz and Ivey, in press).

Drum and Knott (1977) surveyed nineteen systematic programs now being used in counseling centers throughout the country. All are designed to meet specific behavioral objectives. Systematic programs have both cognitive and affective components. They utilize and incorporate an "educational-experiential format, goal orientation, and systematic-sequential approaches to resolution of a problem situation" (p. 14). Ivey's microcounseling program provides a structured experience combining video feedback and a learning format for teaching twelve behavioral skills (Ivey, 1971). Rathus (1973) developed an assertiveness training program for women that used a group format to teach nine specific behaviors. Uhlemann (1968) provided a method that systematically brings together an experiential encounter and behavior change. Other systematic training programs designed to achieve desired behavior change include Ellis' Rational Emotive Therapy adapted by Maultsby (1970); the basic communications-skills program developed by Pierce and Drasgow (1969); the systematic Step Group Therapy Program developed by Authier (1973); the Community-Reinforcement Alcohol Treatment Program developed by Hunt and Azrin (1973); and the Human Relations Training Program at the Houston Veterans Administration Hospital developed by Hanson, Rothous, O'Connell, and Wiggins (1969).

It becomes evident from this review that many dimensions of psychological theory are pointing to systematic training as a way to change behavior, as well as to meet the growing demand for services. Systematic training also supports the learning of skills in a developmental process.

The movement of the helping fields toward systematic training is extremely significant for programs dealing with White awareness. It has become evident that many of the techniques previously used were haphazard. If White attitudes changed as a result of cognitive or affective programs, it is still unclear whether any change occurred in White behavior. Given the lack of techniques available to deal with White racism, and the conclusion that systematic training produces desired results (Authier, Gustafson, Guerney, and Kasdorf, 1975), it appears likely that this form of training can in fact change White people's racist attitudes and behaviors. Such a training program is presented in this book.

CHAPTER 3

How to Use This Program

This chapter provides the facilitator with an overview of the White-on-White systematic training program.

Objectives and Goals

The over-all objectives of the program are to help Whites become aware of how racism affects their lives and to help them change their racist attitudes and behaviors. The program strives to help Whites understand that racism in the United States is a White problem and that being White implies being racist. This understanding is achieved most successfully through (1) confrontation—identifying the discrepancies that exist between what one says and what one does—and (2) a reeducation process—examining history and perspectives through new perceptual filters. If participants can recognize the inconsistencies between ideologies and behaviors at institutional and cultural levels, they can better understand how their own attitudes and behaviors have been permeated by racism. Once Whites become aware of this dimension, they will more easily own their racism and develop ways to combat it.

Unlike many racism awareness programs, this program is not designed to produce guilt or to confront people in a way that "puts them down." Guilt often serves to entrench people in their attitudes —to keep them feeling sorry for themselves or others. This program is designed to help White people become free of the perspectives that have trapped them in their views of themselves and in their interactions with other Whites and with members of minority groups.

Once participants have developed an awareness of the problem of racism on institutional, cultural, and individual levels, it is critical that their behavior also change in line with that awareness. One helpful way to produce that desired behavioral change has been used by Uhlemann (1968) with encounter groups. The participants developed an objective before a marathon group experience. The objective was a specific behavioral change. I have also used this approach successfully in this program. Once participants found that they could change one small behavior, the fear of making further changes lessened.

They could then recognize the choices they had about their own behavior and begin to combat racism on a personal as well as an institutional level.

This program consists of six stages of development and appropriate exercises to work through each stage. If the goals of this program are reached, by the end of the workshop the participants will be able to:

1. Name and clearly define the concepts of bias, bigotry, prejudice, and racism.
2. Describe and examine racism in its institutional, cultural, and individual forms.
3. Identify and articulate personal feelings and fears around the issue of racism.
4. Define ways in which one's own attitudes and behaviors are representative of racism in the United States.
5. Develop and act on specific strategies designed to combat racism on an institutional and individual level.

Assumptions

The following assumptions form the basis of this training program:

Racism is a predominantly White problem. Therefore, being White in America implies being racist. White people are responsible for the perpetuation of White racism in a White racist system.

All Americans have feelings and thoughts on the issue of racism. Virtually no person of any racial group in the United States can grow up without being exposed to and developing some prejudiced attitudes about another person or group. Whites, being part of a White racist system, have many unresolved thoughts, feelings, and questions centering around the dynamics and issues of racism. Socially and psychologically, racism prevents Whites from escaping from ethnocentrism. In the White world Whites subconsciously learn to fear and reject human beings who differ from them (Citron, 1969). Such emotions affect their relationships with others, as well as their own mental health.

White people can learn about racism with other White people. Racist attitudes are often developed without any personal exposure to Third World people. Therefore, Whites can begin the process of learning about racism with other Whites who have begun to explore their own racism. This approach avoids exploiting Third World people for White people's learning.

Whites need to be reeducated. They have grown up in a system that has ingrained in them racist ideologies and attitudes. They need to be in a trusting climate in which they can strip away some of these old ideologies and perceptions and become open to the realities of racism cognitively and emotionally. This will enable them to understand themselves better as White people, as well as to explore their role in combating racism in American society.

It is physically, socially, and psychologically advantageous for Whites to learn about racism for their own survival. As Welsing (1972) emphasizes, Whites make up only one-tenth of the world's population; Third World people constitute the other nine-tenths. Most of the natural resources are contained within the Third World countries. In the next few decades the world's wealth may be redistributed into the Third World countries. For their own survival, physical and economic, Whites must change their racist system and attitudes so that they can peacefully exist with all Third World peoples. It has also been pointed out that racism is mentally unhealthy for White people. On a humanistic level it is in White people's best interest to learn about and deal with their racism.

This program is a step in a process and not an end in itself. One of the things learned from the Woman's Movement is that it is essential for women and men to spend some time in same-sex groups in order to explore their perspectives in a supportive environment. They are then better able to improve relationships with the other sex. This has been seen as well with White and Third World groups. If Whites are in a setting in which they can develop their consciousness of their whiteness and their racism, they can then move toward developing relationships with other Whites and Third World people that are more aware and humanistic and less oppressive. This training program is a step in that direction. Clearly one training program cannot alleviate all of one's racism. It serves as one dimension of this process.

Out of these assumptions this training program was developed and was designed to help make Whites more aware of racism and to provide mechanisms by which they can move in a more positive and healthy direction.

Content and Process—A Word to the Facilitator

To use this program effectively, the facilitator should keep in mind several key factors. Above all, the facilitator should have a good understanding of racism. This includes both an awareness on a personal level of your own prejudices and assumptions and an ability to analyze and describe racism on an institutional and cultural level. To try to facilitate this program—or any program dealing with racism —without a good understanding and working knowledge of the dynamics of racism not only will cause the program to be ineffective but also may perpetuate the participants' racism, as well as your own.

You should be open to your own learning needs and should be a role model whose ideas, attitudes, and values can be tested by individuals and the group. Your willingness to disclose your grapplings with your own racism and the areas that are still unresolved for you will be most helpful in the learning process of others. The facilitator who is a role model will help participants in their own self-examination. It is critical to remember that racism runs deep and that we can never be completely cured of the disease. What we can do is control that part of us and not let it control us.

The facilitator should also have a solid base of group-process skills. A climate of trust must be established so that participants feel safe in exploring their attitudes and behaviors and comfortable in disclosing them to the group. It is essential for the facilitator to recognize how difficult it is for most White people to come to grips with their racism. Therefore, support, caring, and concern for the participants in this experience are critical. While dealing with the content issues—for example, those defining racism or exploring institutional racism—the facilitator must also be aware of the process issues—how people are feeling, how they respond to one another, and so on. Both are necessary for an effective program. It will be useful to read through the entire program before using it, so that you can get a clear picture of both the content and the possible process issues that may emerge.

It is essential to remember that this program is a beginning, not an end. It is designed to give participants an in-depth view of racism and to help them begin to explore and come to understand White racism on cognitive and affective levels with the support of other White people. From there the participants can continue to explore each form of racism and become actively involved in developing ways

25

to combat it. As a result of this experience White people can come to accept their whiteness. They can then develop relationships with both Whites and members of other races that are nonexploitive and nonoppressive. This training program thus represents a first step in uncovering the deeply rooted disease racism and a first step in the direction of liberation for all people.

Format

The six stages of the training program are contained in Part II of this book. Each stage is presented in the following format: (1) an introduction, followed by sections on rationale and method, and (2) the exercises themselves. A list of exercises faces the opening page of each stage. Materials used in the exercises (questionnaires, forms, and so on) follow the discussion of the exercise. Resources for each stage are given in the Appendix.

Stage 1 lays the groundwork for participants to understand racism in society and in themselves. In this first stage the key concepts prejudice and racism are explored. The participants become aware of the reality that *power* is the major factor differentiating racism and prejudice.

Stage 2 probes institutional racism. Participants are further confronted with the discrepancies in American ideology and behavior.

Stage 3 is designed to help participants sort through some of the feelings and reactions that were triggered in the previous stages. Feelings of fear, projection and guilt are brought to the surface.

Stage 4 explores cultural racism, including an examination of language, music, norms, and values. Attention is focused on White ethnocentrism and cultural differences.

Stage 5 centers around the meaning of whiteness and helps participants claim their White identity as an essential part of themselves. In this stage participants explore their own prejudices and personal roles in supporting racism.

Stage 6 helps participants develop specific action strategies to combat personal and institutional racism and define their next steps in becoming anti-racist (Katz and Ivey, 1977).

A list of recommended articles, books, and pamphlets is given for each stage. These materials should be used in conjunction with the exercises to achieve maximum effectiveness.

The Appendix presents an array of resources, including films, tapes, pamphlets, organizations, and agencies, that are useful to the learning process.

Groups: Why All White?

As explained earlier, this program is designed to be used with all-White groups so that the participants can:

1. Establish a climate that focuses on the meaning of being White and on developing a sense of whiteness as part of one's identity;
2. Explore their racist attitudes and behaviors in a climate of trust and support;
3. Accomplish this learning without exploiting minority people as the "teachers."

Facilitators

This program can be staffed in a number of ways. It can be facilitated by one person or by cotrainers. The staff must have a deep understanding of the issue of racism. It is useful to have a female-male team and to draw analogies to the Woman's Movement where possible. The program can be cofacilitated by an interracial team, though there is the risk that participants will assume that the minority person speaks for all minorities or that the group will constantly be asking the minority leader about his or her experiences with racism. The interracial team is usable if both facilitators can use these dynamics for the group's learning. It is essential to keep a watchful eye on that part of the process.

Designs: Application to Your Setting

This program can be used and applied in many contexts and formats, depending upon the setting and the time limitations. The key to an effective program is to maintain flexibility and adaptability. A little imagination and knowledge of the group's needs is vital. The more the content of the program focuses on issues that reflect the participants' world, the more investment they will probably make, and the greater will be the degree of learning. Whether you are working with teachers, business people, counselors, administrators, students, church groups, or government officials, the program is easily adaptable. Some of the exercises presented in the handbook were geared to a university setting as only one example of the program's many applications. It has been adapted and used as part of Affirmative Action programs; in school systems with teachers, counselors, and administrators; in university settings with students, faculty, and dormitory staffs.

Given the focus on racism and the systematic nature of the program, many of the experiences are usable in any setting. It will be most important to use your participants' context in Stage 2. For example, in using Exercise 9, "Mini-Lecture: Kinds and Levels of Racism," you would discuss the different levels with examples from your setting. In Exercise 12 the simulation role play similarly should reflect issues in the participants' environment.

Using experiences adapted to your group's needs, together with the systematic stage-by-stage process, will assure maximum effectiveness. The first task is to help participants open the perceptual door and pull off the blinders that they often wear. Once they can begin to identify racism in institutions, the culture, and themselves, they can expand that awareness. Therefore, the specific focus that is used—school, business, academic community, church, and so on—becomes less important than developing the understanding of the underlying dimensions of racism. The setting is essentially a vehicle by which to develop that awareness.

Formats

The program has been used in various formats, ranging from three-hour introductory sessions to forty-five-hour semester-long university courses. Often all that can be provided within the time limits are short introductory sessions. I have facilitated three-hour segments that concentrate on Stage 1 concepts. These can provide a step for some to begin to explore their attitudes. It is usually a door opener, no more. I have often experienced a high degree of personal frustration in such sessions. If you can be clear and realistic about goals—that is, to be content to raise the issue of racism and help participants begin to explore it—you will probably lessen your own frustration. When you are using Stage 1 experiences only, it is essential, to go slowly and avoid making participants defensive. That is a difficult task in a short, one-time workshop. The hope is that you can create enough concern that the participants will continue to probe the issue on their own.

One-day, eight-hour sessions can be expanded to include institutional issues in Stage 2 and some strategy planning in Stage 6. One popular design, which has been used with in-service and preservice teachers, includes Exercises 3, 6, 8 (Stage 1), 9, 14, 18 (Stage 2), and 43 and 46 (Stage 6). These exercises help establish definitions, give teachers some awareness of institutional racism in the educational process, and help them develop ways to utilize that learning in their classrooms. The more time you have, of course, the more effective your program will be.

More exercises have been included than can probably be used in any one workshop. Although times are given for each exercise, they are approximations only, and many can be shorter or longer, depending on how participants respond and how involved they become. No matter what combination of exercises you use, it is important to follow the systematic process. For example, to start at Stage 4 and then go back to Stage 1 will probably not prove useful to participants' learning. It is important to consider the level of sophistication and experience of your group. You may need to spend only a short time on Stage 1 and 2 and concentrate on the other stages. You should know your group and identify what will fit their consciousness.

In developing your design, try to plan for time between sessions to allow your participants to reflect on and integrate the materials and concepts. I often provide Stage 1 reading materials before beginning the program. In this way participants can begin thinking and raising questions in their minds.

Finally, plan for some follow-up sessions. The more reinforcement participants have the more they may be able to change. It is difficult to become anti-racist in a racist system. Your participants will need support to make changes in and around themselves. Structure that reinforcement into the design and impress upon the participants the need for support. Ongoing task forces and support groups often develop as a result.

Measuring Program Effectiveness

One of the problems involved in any form of training is determining its effectiveness. A question often asked, particularly of racism training is, Are White people really changing, or are they merely becoming more knowledgeable racists? I am convinced that awareness is not enough. It is behavior that counts. My charge to the user of this program is to impress upon participants the importance of changing not merely attitudes but also behavior. Stokely Carmichael's adage, "If you're not part of the solution, you're part of the problem," still holds, as does, "Inaction is action."

My rule of thumb is that if participants are involved six months later in some positive new behavior, the program can be considered effective. In the school setting such behavior can range from teaching short courses or offering workshops to changing curricula in schools to reflect a multicultural perspective.

When measuring the degree of effectiveness of the program, I have used such instruments as the Steckler Anti-Black and Anti-White Scales (Steckler, 1957) and the Attitude Exploration Survey (Adams, 1973) to assess attitude change and the Behavioral Rating Scale (Uhlemann, 1968) to measure behavior change. By these scales, as well as the subjective evaluations of leaders and participants, the program is measurably successful. Whatever means are used, it is essential to evaluate both the participants' growth and the facilitator's own effectiveness.

A Final Note

In dealing with racism, keep in mind its complexity, its pervasiveness, and its entrenchment in White society. Change often comes slowly. Participants may leave the program with little or no apparent change in their perspectives but in time begin to see racism and themselves in a new light. The process of developing awareness, accepting and owning one's whiteness, and developing ways to change is a difficult task. The facilitator's job is to help Whites take the first steps in that process.

PART TWO The Training Program

Stage 1   Racism: Definitions and Inconsistencies

Exercise 1   Establishing Goals and Objectives   page 37

2   Concentric Circles: Getting to Know One
Another   38

3   Definition of Prejudice   40
Prejudice Definition Sheet   42

4   Exploring Prejudice: *Black Thumb*   43

5   Exploring Prejudice: *The Friendly Game*   44

6   Designing a Racist Community   46

7   Fuzzy Concept: Racism   48

8   Definition of Racism   49
Racism Definition Sheet   51

See Appendix, pages 186 and 197, for readings and resources for Stage 1.

32

Stage 1 Racism: Definitions and Inconsistencies

Stage 1 is a crucial step in the reeducation of White people. It lays the groundwork for participants to explore racism in society and in themselves. To achieve this end, it is necessary to:

1. Help people feel comfortable in the group, get to know one another, and develop trust.
2. Help them discover and define key terminology basic to understanding the dynamics of racism.
3. Help them name and begin exploring inconsistencies in society.

All the exercises in this stage have been developed to meet these objectives.

Given the objectives, Stage 1 appears to be a formidable challenge. Participants usually enter this stage with different levels of awareness as a result of their assumptions, perceptions, and personal experiences with racism. It is necessary to meet them where they are, as well as to develop an atmosphere that ensures that they can work together. Stage 1 attempts to help participants get to know one another and feel comfortable. In the first few warm-up exercises they share their perspectives in order to develop that climate and commonality.

The defining process is one of the most important steps in understanding racism. Many participants use the words *bias, bigotry, prejudice,* and *racism* interchangeably, assuming that there is no difference in meaning. It is vital that each of these terms be clearly defined so that participants can distinguish among them. In this way they will have the foundation and reference base necessary to explore racism and the way it operates in American society. Many of the exercises in Stage 1 focus on the defining process to facilitate the further exploration of institutional and individual racism in later stages.

It is also important that participants be able to look at their own beliefs, attitudes, and values and see how they act upon them. Anoth-

33

er part of this stage is thus designed to highlight the inconsistencies that exist between words and actions. Because it is easier at first to look outside ourselves when dealing with racism, inconsistencies are explored in terms of the society's values and attitudes, which are then compared with actual behavior. This survey lays a groundwork for later stages, in which participants explore their own ideologies and behaviors for inconsistencies.

The participants explore America's ideologies, such as: "All people are created equal"; "America is a land of equal opportunity"; "You can make it if you try"; and "Liberty and justice for all." Then they confront the reality that in fact these beliefs are not matched by actions. This learning is basic to an awareness of the "American dilemma." Gunnar Myrdal (1944) described it as

> the deep cultural and psychological conflict among the American people of: American ideals of equality, freedom, God given dignity of the individual, inalienable rights on the one hand, against practices of discrimination, humiliation, insult, denial of opportunity to Negroes and others in a racist society on the other.

This stage names the American dilemma. Awareness of inconsistencies is then further developed in each stage as a crucial aspect of each participant's learning.

Method   As a facilitator you will be working on three levels. This makes your task very different from, and perhaps more difficult than, leading a nonspecific issue-oriented group, such as a T-group. In this particular group you will need to deal with:

1. The climate of the group.
2. Content vis à vis racism.
3. Your own issues of racism.

It is important to be aware that this is probably the first time this group has come together to deal with the issue of racism in a structured experience. Therefore, the facilitator must be sensitive to issues in a "new group" in addition to the content of the program. It is necessary to develop trust and a supportive climate. One way to accomplish this is through the initial exercises in Stage 1. A second mechanism is through the support of the facilitator. That support might include *not* processing racist language and remarks throughout

34

Stage 1. Clearly, around an issue such as racism people will be unwilling to share their real, innermost feelings and attitudes if they do not feel the support of the group and the facilitator. By processing participants' racism in Stage 1, the facilitator may shut them off. Racist remarks and language, such as discussion of "reverse racism," racist jokes, and/or expressions such as "blacklisting," and "black sheep" should be noted and processed at a point when participants can hear the comments and understand them. What is important in this first stage is that the facilitator begins to develop a climate of trust and support. The degree of rapport that the facilitator has with the group, as well as the feeling in the group itself, will either help or seriously hinder the learning of the participants.

A second aspect of facilitating the group pertains to the content issues. The first stage concentrates on external issues—participants are engaged intellectually in exploring definitions and societal inconsistencies. They are steered away from exploring personal racism, because at the outset it is easier for them to look at issues outside themselves. Once they begin to understand what racism is and how it operates in society, they can then more adequately and honestly explore their own racism.

Another Stage 1 dynamic directly related to the issue of racism is the participants' questions about how they can deal with racism in an all-White group. Here the facilitator must take an active role (if no one else in the group does), pointing out that many White people have developed their racist attitudes without having had any contact with Third World people and that, therefore, through various mechanisms the participants can explore their racism without the presence of Third World people. The facilitator should emphasize these points: In many instances of Third World–White groups the Third World people are exploited. White people learn from them about racism—but what do the Third World people learn? The question becomes, Who would benefit if the group were mixed, and at whose expense?

In this stage—and in succeeding ones as well—the facilitator must take an active role. In Stage 1 that role includes pressing for understanding and acceptance of the definitions of racism and prejudice.

The third, and perhaps the most difficult, task of the facilitator involves his or her own role in the process. The facilitator should be knowledgeable in dealing with racism as a White problem. That includes being aware of one's own racism, understanding the process of racism, and being committed to continuing to learn about his or her own racism. It is crucial that the facilitator discuss this with the group, making it clear that in fact she or he is not *the* expert on racism and moreover cannot speak for Third World people. The role of the facilitator is to help other White people begin to understand what racism is and to find some ways to combat it. This learning is ideally a continuous process for all members of the group. The facilitator thus has the complex task of not only facilitating participants' growth and development but also remaining open for his or her own learning.

The content and process issues summarized above are the basis for Stage 1, and ultimately for all stages in the program. The pages that follow set forth the specific mechanisms, exercises, and resources necessary for the development of the first stage.

Exercise 1   Establishing Goals and Objectives

1. To help participants feel comfortable in the group.   **Goals**
2. To understand some of the participants' differing expectations.

None   **Materials needed**

1. Have the group sit in a circle.   **Instructions**
2. Ask the participants to share:
   a. Their names.
   b. Their reasons for participating in the workshop.
   c. Their expectations for the workshop.
3. Share your (the facilitator's) own expectations for the workshop:
   a. Participants will take responsibility for themselves and the group.
   b. Participants will try to share their feelings and be as honest as possible.

Any form of expectation-sharing exercise would be useful. You may   **Note to facilitator**
want to begin with an experience that simply serves to get people
acquainted and then follow with a separate experience to share expectations.

10 to 15 minutes (all times noted apply to groups of twelve to fifteen **Time**
persons)

Exercise 2   Concentric Circles: Getting to Know One Another[1]

Goals
1. To help participants begin to raise the issue of racism.
2. To begin developing a climate of trust and support.

Materials needed

None

Instructions
1. Have the group count off by twos (*1-2-1-2*).
2. a. Ask all the ones to sit in a circle with their backs to the center of the circle.
   b. Ask all the twos to sit in an outside circle, facing the ones (each person has a partner facing her or him).
3. Ask all the ones to share with the person opposite them:
   a. Their names.
   b. "Something special that happened to me this week."
   This process should continue for about two minutes.
4. Ask all the twos to repeat the same process.
5. Ask all the twos to move one person to the right.
6. Have them repeat the above process, sharing names and responding to "one feeling I have about being here."
7. Continue this process for another two to four rounds, always asking twos to move one person to the right. Some of the other exchanges that may be asked for include:
   a. "Share the first word that comes to your mind when you think about racism."
   b. "Share one experience you have had with racism and how you responded."
   c. "Share one feeling you have about dealing with racism."

---

[1] Adapted from an exercise developed by Gerald Weinstein, School of Education, University of Massachusetts.

It is important to keep your ears open to the issues that participants
bring to the group. Particularly observe the questions that deal specifically with racism.

20 to 30 minutes   **Time**

Exercise 3   Definition of Prejudice

Goals
1. To help participants begin to understand prejudice.
2. To develop a functional definition of prejudice.

Materials needed
Prejudice Definition Sheet (page 42)
Newsprint
Felt markers
Masking tape

Instructions
1. Begin the exercise by stating that it is essential to understand the differences between racism and prejudice before exploring how they operate in our society. Then begin to explore the definition of prejudice.
2. Pass out copies of the Prejudice Definition Sheet.
3. Ask the participants to look at the four definitions presented on the sheet. Using the four as a starting point, ask them to develop a definition of prejudice with which they each feel comfortable.
4. Divide the group into small groups of four.
5. Ask the participants to share their individual definitions in the small groups and then develop a group definition of prejudice. Ask someone in each group to jot down the definition on newsprint.
6. After fifteen minutes ask each group to hang up its newsprint and share its definition with the large group.
7. Reactions, discussion. Points raised should include the following:
   a. Prejudice is based on assumptions that have not been checked out.
   b. The word *prejudice* is composed of *pre* and *judge*. This is a key concept in understanding prejudice.
   c. It is important to understand the difference between prejudice and bias.

This exercise begins to highlight the key dynamics of prejudice and begins distinguishing prejudice from racism. You may want to include a mini-lecture on the difference between prejudice and bias. A good resource is Pat Bidol, "Mini-Lecture on the Difference Between Prejudice and Racism" (see Appendix). **Note to facilitator**

25 minutes **Time**

Prejudice Definition Sheet

According to the *Random House Dictionary of the English Language* (1967):

prejudice

1. An unfavorable opinion or feeling formed beforehand or without knowledge, thought, or reason.
2. Any preconceived opinion or feeling, either favorable or unfavorable.
3. Unreasonable feelings, opinions, or attitudes, especially of a hostile nature, directed against a racial, religious, or national group.

To these definitions may be added:

4. Negative personal behavior that discriminates against individuals of such a group.

Exercise 4   Exploring Prejudice: *Black Thumb*

To further define prejudice and how it functions.

Goal

Film *Black Thumb* (page 197)[1]
16-mm movie projector
Screen

**Materials
needed**

1. Show the film *Black Thumb*.

Instructions

2. Stop the film halfway through. Ask the participants to share what they have observed and the assumptions made by themselves and by those in the film.
3. Ask the participants to share what they have observed in the film and any assumptions they may have made.
4. Ask the participants to project what will happen next.
5. Show the rest of the film.
6. Reactions, discussion. Questions raised should include:
   a. How do we stereotype each other?
   b. How do our assumptions and preconceived ideas about one another foster prejudice?
7. Ask the participants to brainstorm specific examples of prejudiced behavior.
8. Ask the participants to brainstorm inconsistencies in behavior that they observed in the film.

15 minutes

Time

[1] This film may be used alone, as a substitute for Exercise 5, or in addition to Exercise 5.

43

Exercise 5   Exploring Prejudice: *The Friendly Game*

Goal   To explore Black-White relations and how they function in relation to prejudice.

Materials needed

Film *The Friendly Game* (page 197)[1]
16-mm movie projector
Screen

Instructions

1. Show the film *The Friendly Game.*
2. Stop the film halfway through.
3. Ask the participants to share what they have seen and the assumptions that they have made. Ask them to share also any feelings that they may have about either man.
4. Ask the participants to project what will happen next.
5. Show the rest of the film.
6. Reactions, discussion. Questions raised should include the following:
    a. What attitudes does each man bring to the game?
    b. What assumptions does each man make about the other?
    c. How do these attitudes and assumptions affect each man's behavior?
    d. What is the White man doing?
    e. What is the Black man doing?
    f. Who has the power in this film?
    g. What kind of power is it?
    h. How does this film relate to society?

---

[1] This film may be used alone, as a substitute for Exercise 4, or in addition to Exercise 4.

It is important to process the film, focusing on assumptions and atti-   **Note to**
tudes in order to explore prejudice and how it operates. It may be   **facilitator**
helpful to show the film again in a later stage. At that time you can
concentrate on other dimensions of the film. With the film comes a
film guide that highlights key dimensions for processing.

25 minutes   **Time**

Exercise 6   Designing a Racist Community[1]

Goals   1. To identify the key elements of racism.
2. To discover how racism functions in our society.

Materials needed   Newsprint
Felt markers
Masking tape

Instructions   1. Divide the group into small groups of four to six persons. Give each group newsprint and felt markers.
2. Ask the groups to design a racist community. Have each group describe its community on newsprint. It can be blatantly racist or subtly racist. Ask the groups to make sure they describe:
   a. The makeup of the community.
   b. Who makes the decisions.
   c. How the decisions are made.
   d. Who has control of money.
   e. Who sets up the formal policy of the community.
   f. Who sets up the informal policy of the community.
   g. The roles of the various institutions of the community—schools, churches, businesses, media, social organizations, recreational facilities.
3. Put up the sheets of newsprint and ask each group to share its community with the whole group.
4. Reactions, discussion. Points raised should include the following:
   a. What are the key elements that make your community and all the others racist? List these elements separately on a sheet of newsprint headed "Racism Is . . ." (this list will be used in Exercise 10).

[1]Design created by Duke Harris, Pat Bidol, and Dan Kirchbaum.

b. How different is your community from real communities in the United States?

c. Review the elements the groups listed in their designs of a racist community. Focus on the power issue—Whites have the power to oppress Third World people in this country, but Third World people do not have the power to oppress Whites.

Note to facilitator

1. This is one of the most important exercises of this series. It generates a lot of data that you will constantly be using throughout this stage and the succeeding stages.

2. Before processing, you should discuss the importance of this exercise. Emphasize that it is necessary to be aware of and able to pinpoint clearly what racism is—that is, how it functions—before we can begin to combat racism. We must know exactly what we are trying to fight in order to fight it effectively.

3. During the exercise you should go from group to group to observe the process. It may be helpful to keep a record of individuals' ideologies to feed back to them at a later date.

4. During this exercise there is often a tendency for participants to try to make Third World people the oppressors by putting Third World people in the majority and reversing the actual roles that White people and Third World people take on in our society. It is extremely important to note this in processing the exercise: Why do people try to deny the role of Whites in this country? Does this really happen in the United States? If so, how? Do Third World people have power in this country? What kind of power? Where does it exist? It is essential that participants begin to look at their ownership of and responsibility for racism. This exercise begins to clarify the reality that Whites are responsible for racism and that Third World people do not have the social, economic, or political power to be racist against Whites as a group in the United States.

5. This exercise also helps participants begin exploring inconsistencies in American society. The behaviors listed on the newsprint sheet entitled "Racism Is . . ." will prove helpful in Exercise 10, "Naming and Discovering Inconsistencies."

2 hours (1 hour to design, 1 hour to process)   **Time**

Exercise 7   Fuzzy Concept: Racism[1]

Goal   To clarify further the elements of racism.

Materials needed   Paper (newsprint)
Pens or pencils (or felt markers)

Instructions
1. Ask the participants to draw a circle with lines radiating from it.
2. In the middle of the circle write the word *racism*.
3. Ask the participants to free-associate with the word *racism* and write their responses at the end of each line.
4. Share the wheels in the large group.

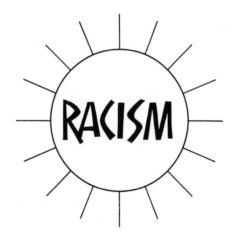

Time   15 to 20 minutes

[1]Adapted from an exercise developed by Alice Sargeant. Reproduced by permission from *Beyond Sex Roles* by Alice Sargeant, copyright © 1977 West Publishing Company. All rights reserved.

Exercise 8   Definition of Racism

1. To develop a functional definition of racism.
2. To clarify the differences between racism and prejudice.

Racism Definition Sheet (page 51)
Newsprint
Felt markers
Masking tape

1. Hand out copies of the Racism Definition Sheet.
2. Ask the participants to look at the five definitions presented on the sheet. Using them as a starting point, ask the participants to develop their own definitions of racism.
3. Divide the group into small groups of four.
4. Ask the participants to share their individual definitions in the small groups and then develop a group definition of racism. Ask someone in the group to write the definition on newsprint.
5. After fifteen minutes ask each group to display its definition and share it with the large group.
6. Reactions, discussion. Points raised should include the following:
   a. What seems to be common to all the definitions?
   b. Is power part of your group's definition? If not, how does your definition differ from prejudice?
   c. What is power, and how do you define it (in institutional, political, or economic terms)?
   d. Who has the power in our society? (If necessary, refer to the racist communities designed in Exercise 6).
   e. By the definition of racism, are Third World people racist in America today against Whites?
   f. Do Third World people presently have the power to oppress Whites?

49

Note to   1. Refer again to the definition of prejudice and differentiate it from
facilitator   racism. By the end of this exercise these two terms should have
distinct meanings for the participants.

2. It is important to push for the understanding that racism is *prejudice plus power* and that, therefore, Third World people cannot be racist against Whites in the United States. Third World people can be prejudiced against Whites, but clearly they do not have the power to enforce that prejudice. Although participants may not at this point totally accept this view or feel comfortable with it, it is important to establish the concept as a working definition. As the course progresses, it will, it is hoped, be better understood by participants.

Time   30 minutes

Racism Definition Sheet

According to the *Random House Dictionary of the English Language* (1967):

racism

1. A belief that human races have distinctive characteristics that determine their respective cultures, usually involving the idea that one's own race is superior and has the right to rule others.
2. A policy of enforcing such asserted right.
3. A system of government and society based upon it.

To these definitions may be added:

4. Perpetuation of belief in the superiority of the White race.
5. Prejudice plus power.

Stage 2　Confronting the Reality of Racism

Exercise　9　Mini-Lecture: Kinds and Levels of Racism　page 55
　　　　　10　Naming and Discovering Inconsistencies:
　　　　　　　　An American Dilemma　59
　　　　　　　　Commonly Listed Ideologies and Slogans　60
　　　　　11　The Web of Institutional Racism: A Simu-
　　　　　　　　lation Game　61
　　　　　12　Institutional Racism at Work: A Simulation
　　　　　　　　Experience　63
　　　　　　　　Simulation Design 1: College Setting　65
　　　　　　　　Simulation Design 2: Public School
　　　　　　　　Setting　67
　　　　　13　The Drawbridge　70
　　　　　　　　"The Drawbridge"　72
　　　　　14　*Black History: Lost, Stolen, or Strayed*　73
　　　　　15　The Web of Institutional Racism　75
　　　　　16　The Effects of Institutional Racism on
　　　　　　　　Native Americans　77
　　　　　17　Debate　78
　　　　　18　Some Perspectives on Institutional Racism　80
　　　　　19　In-Depth Exploration of Institutional Racism
　　　　　　　　in Specific Institutions: Projects　82
　　　　　　　　"Inventory of Racism"　83
　　　　　20　More Perspectives on Institutional Racism　89
　　　　　21　Reality Testing: How Much Have I Been
　　　　　　　　Cheated in My Education?　90

See Appendix, pages 188 and 197, for readings and resources for Stage 2.

Stage 2   Confronting the Reality of Racism

The focus of Stage 1 was developing an understanding of prejudice **Introduction**
and racism by establishing clear definitions. Stage 2 elaborates on
the definition of racism by exploring the specifics of institutional
racism. The exercises in this second stage are designed to:

1. Confront participants with institutional racism.
2. Begin to reeducate participants about the functioning of racism
   in institutions.
3. Highlight inconsistencies between institutional values and attitudes and institutional behaviors.

So that participants will truly comprehend racism as a predominantly **Rationale**
White problem, they must be confronted with and become aware of
the depth and breadth of racism in American society. Stage 2 seeks
to explore in detail how deeply racism is ingrained in us from birth
onward and how it operates in every institutional system.

The exercises in this section are extremely diversified so that each
participant can begin to see the reality of institutional racism. Some
of the exercises permit participants to experience oppression, on a
very small scale, through simulation. Others expose participants to
the perspectives of Third World people who have experienced the
effects of racism. Still other exercises illustrate how White people
benefit from institutional racism, as well as how they are trapped by
it. Participants will also be engaged in discovering for themselves
how institutional racism functions. In each exercise is one essential
element: a focus on inconsistencies. It is essential to point up the
inconsistencies between the values and attitudes of American institutions and their actual behavior. Once Whites can see the discrepancies between the two, they can better determine the positive steps
that need to be taken to close the gaps.

In Stage 2 many crucial issues are explored. This stage further
clarifies and expands on the functional definitions developed in Stage
1. Stage 2 is concerned with exploring in depth the American dilemma: inconsistencies in American institutions; the issue of power;

"blaming the victim"—that is, negating the White problem; the responsibility of White people for institutional racism; and the reality that "reverse racism" does not exist in America today. The exercises are designed to help clarify these issues and present some new perspectives and data to participants so that they can more fully comprehend the dynamics of White racism.

Method   Stage 2 presents a number of challenges to the facilitator. It can prove to be an extremely emotional stage for the participants. They may find themselves feeling confused, overwhelmed, unprepared to deal with all the new data. It is important to keep these feelings at a manageable level but not to discharge them completely. In Stage 3 all these feelings will be intensified. One way to manage feelings of guilt is to emphasize that racism is deeply ingrained in our system and that we are clearly products of our system. Thus it should not come as a surprise that we as White people are racist. The question will become, at a later stage, What can we do about it?

An important dynamic to try to achieve in the group during this stage is ownership of racism as a White problem, including some acceptance of responsibility to make changes in the system to combat it.

It is also crucial to focus on White people's behavior. The group may often attempt to change the focus of the discussion to identify instances and systems of Third World "racism" ("reverse racism"). It is important to process this reaction and discuss the group's need for flight from some of the real issues of racism in American society and from a close look at the American system as a whole, in which White racism is pervasive.

It is important for the facilitator to serve as a confronter in this stage. The facilitator's job is to highlight hard realities about racism and discrepancies in the participants, at the same time avoiding "coming down" on them. In this stage participants are challenged to begin to examine the world around them—the institutions that nurtured their development.

Exercise 9   Mini-Lecture: Kinds and Levels of Racism

1. To deepen participants' understanding of the definition of racism **Goals**
   developed in Stage 1 by pinpointing the different kinds and levels
   of racism.
2. To move participants from Stage 1 to Stage 2, which is concerned
   with exploring institutional racism.

Chart below on newsprint (or chalkboard)   **Materials**
Masking tape   **needed**

1. The following chart can serve as a guide in discussing the different   **Instructions**
   kinds and levels of racism. Display it on newsprint and refer to it
   while giving the mini-lecture.

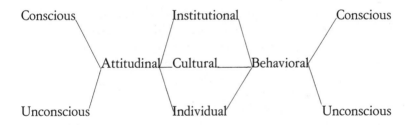

Conscious   Institutional   Conscious

Attitudinal—Cultural——Behavioral

Unconscious   Individual   Unconscious

2. Follow the outline below in developing the mini-lecture.

I. Kinds of racism
   A. Institutional
      1. Education
      2. Economics
      3. Health services
      4. Politics
      5. Housing

B. Cultural
   1. Music
   2. Religion
   3. Standards, needs, norms
   4. Aesthetics
   5. Language

C. Individual
   1. Attitudes
   2. Behaviors
   3. Socialization
   4. Self-interest
   5. Interaction

II. Levels of racism
   A. Conscious level
      1. Institutional racist attitudes
         a. Belief in limited intellectual abilities of minority children
         b. Belief in stereotypes shown in media
         c. Belief that Affirmative Action is reverse racism
      2. Institutional racist behaviors
         a. Discrimination against minority home buyers by real estate groups fearful of panic selling by Whites
         b. Busing of Black children to White schools
         c. Use of quota systems; tokenism
      3. Individual racist attitudes
         a. Belief in White supremacy
         b. Belief that Blacks are genetically inferior
         c. Belief that Native Americans are savages or alcoholics
      4. Individual racist behaviors
         a. Bombing of Black churches; lynching of Black people
         b. Use of racial epithets ("nigger")
         c. Refusal to integrate or bus White children

   B. Unconscious level
      1. Institutional racist attitudes
         a. Assumption that White personnel can meet the needs of all the people in the institution but that minority staff members can deal only with the needs of other minorities

    b. Disregard of minorities' needs in developing products ("flesh-colored" bandages for White people only)

    c. Disregard of minority cultural perspectives in developing standardized tests

  2. Institutional racist behaviors

    a. Destruction of minority housing in urban renewal to make way for commercial facilities or upper-income housing

    b. Teaching of (White) American history

    c. Consent to the deaths of 500 minority children each year because of lack of proper clothing, shelter, and medical facilities

  3. Individual racist attitudes

    a. Belief in melting-pot theory

    b. Denial of racism ("When I see Black people, I don't see their color—people are people")

    c. Belief that all people are treated equally in the United States

  4. Individual racist behaviors

    a. Laughter at racist jokes

    b. Business dealings with racist companies

    c. Use of anti-Black, pro-White language ("black lie," "white lie")

3. Close the mini-lecture by pointing out that these examples of kinds and levels of racism are but a few illustrations and that others will be identified in subsequent sessions. Emphasize that racism need not be intentional (conscious) but that by their very support of racist institutions and cultural mores Whites are helping perpetuate the racist system.

Note to facilitator

This exercise is useful as a bridge from Stage 1 to Stage 2. At the end of Stage 1 participants may feel lost about where to begin in exploring racism. Now that they have defined racism and have gained some awareness of its pervasiveness, the next step is to begin exploring the dynamics of racism. This mini-lecture serves to present racism in manageable segments. It also helps minimize any anxiety in the group. By discussing racism in terms of kinds and levels, participants usually become open to the issues presented in Stage 2. They see that their exploration will continue to be restricted to areas outside themselves; institutions, not their own behavior, will be investigated. At this stage participants find it easier to blame institutions for racism than to explore their own attitudes and behavior.

In the development of this mini-lecture the following readings from Stage 1 are useful: "Mini-lecture: Difference Between Prejudice and Racism," "Racism Isn't Just . . .," and "White Racism: Definition and Types."

This exercise should be kept short. Specifics of each kind of racism will unfold in subsequent sessions.

If the setting of the group is an educational institution, it might be useful to administer the test discussed in Exercise 21 before conducting this exercise.

Time 10 minutes

Exercise 10   Naming and Discovering Inconsistencies:
An American Dilemma

To explore inconsistencies in society's ideology and behavior   **Goals**

Newsprint   **Materials**
Felt markers   **needed**
Masking tape
Sheet "Racism Is . . ." developed in Exercise 6

1. Divide group into small groups of four to six persons.   **Instructions**
2. Ask each group to brainstorm a list of ideologies and slogans ("All
   people are created equal," "Liberty and justice for all," and so on)
   that the United States professes as part of its basic philosophy.
   Have them write them on newsprint.
3. Ask each group to share its list.
4. In the large group ask participants to name examples of areas in
   which these ideologies are true. You may want to add ideologies
   they omitted (see "Commonly Listed Ideologies and Slogans,"
   page 60).
5. Discuss the implications of inconsistencies and the American
   dilemma.
6. Use the sheet "Racism Is . . .," developed in Exercise 6, to sum up
   inconsistencies in American ideology and behavior. Discuss how
   those inconsistencies foster and perpetuate racism.

This is one of the first exercises in the series dealing specifically with   **Note to**
inconsistencies. Because it is a crucial concept in the development of   **facilitator**
the course, you may wish to ask participants to keep a journal, noting
inconsistencies that they become aware of in society and in themselves.

35 minutes   **Time**

Commonly Listed Ideologies and Slogans

Pull yourself up by your bootstraps.
You can make it if you try.
God created man in his own image.
To get a good job, first get a good education.
First come, first served.
Freedom of the press, freedom of speech.
Do unto others . . . .
Cleanliness is next to godliness.
Government of the people, by the people, for the people.
Free enterprise.
Hard work will equal success.
From rags to riches.
All men are created equal.
Liberty and justice for all.
Land of the free, home of the brave.
In God we trust.
The American dream.
America, the melting pot.
It'll make a man out of you (armed forces).
Live free or die (New Hampshire license plate).
Rights guaranteed under the law.
From sea to shining sea (manifest destiny).
One nation under God.

Exercise 11   The Web of Institutional Racism: A Simulation Game[1]

Goals

1. To help participants begin to understand some of the dynamics of institutional racism by experiencing on a small scale how racism oppresses Third World people.
2. To help participants begin to understand the power behind White racism.

Materials needed

Four staff persons to run the institutions of the simulation: the bank, the university, the employment agency, and the real estate office
Signs for each institution
Play money
Goal sheets for participants
Housing cards
Employment cards
Forms for each institution
Instruction manual for simulation (page 198)

Instructions

This simulation requires a minimum of eighteen participants to be fully effective. At the start of the simulation each participant is given a specific role and a goal that he or she must try to achieve within the six years of the game (each round represents a year). These roles reflect minority people's positions in American society today. All the goals revolve around participants' interactions with the four institutions.

Each institution is operated by a member of the board of directors. This board is responsible for setting up the standards and policies of each institution. In the end the board has the power to decide who "makes it" under the standards and policies it develops. Participants attempt to meet their goals—such as moving into better homes or apartments, getting better jobs, and starting businesses—and find themselves exposed to a system that is frustrating, selective in deter-

[1] Designed by Carole and Charles Camp.

61

mining who receives benefits and gets ahead, and generally oppressive in its treatment of people.

Some participants meet block after block trying to reach their goals, while others get full cooperation from the system. As a result participants experience the injustice of the system and particularly the power that is a basic ingredient of racism. They begin to realize through their own experiences how power can work to maintain the advantage of one group over another. They personally experience a taste of the frustration and anger that is a part of the everyday life of most Third World people.

As a result of these feelings participants will sometimes try to take over or overthrow the institutions, rob the bank, form a new system, or join together. They often gain an understanding of violence (destruction of both property and of individual integrity).

The simulation provides one of the best mechanisms for participants not only to learn about how institutional racism functions but also to experience on a very small scale some of the dynamics of racism and the effects it has on the lives of Third World people. Through the simulation participants can get in touch with some of their personal racism and perhaps question some of their values, in addition to examining overt and covert aspects of institutional racism.

Note to facilitator   If it is not feasible to do this simulation, Exercise 12, "Institutional Racism at Work: A Simulation Experience," confronts participants with some of the same issues.

Time   3 hours

Institutional Racism at Work:
A Simulation Experience[1]

1. To help participants begin to understand some of the dynamics of **Goals**
   institutional racism by experiencing how racism oppresses people.
2. To help participants begin to understand the power in White racism.

Simulation Design 1, College Setting (page 65)   **Materials**
Simulation Design 2, Public School Setting (page 67)   **needed**

1. Assign roles to participants (at least thirteen persons are required **Instructions**
   for Simulation Design 1, eleven for Simulation Design 2). You
   may assign each person's role or let participants choose their parts.
2. Hand out role slips. Read to the group the description of the
   situation so that the setting is clear.
3. Have the groups meet for five minutes to plan their strategies and
   assess their positions.
4. Call the groups together for the meeting. The facilitator serves as
   process observer.
5. Continue the simulation for about forty minutes.
6. Process: Ask the participants to share how they felt in their roles.
   Then share your process notes with the group.

1. You may wish to choose the people who role-play Third World **Note to**
   students, selecting those participants who strongly resist accept- **facilitator**
   ing the definition of racism or who have trouble understanding why
   Third World people need and/or want their own cultures.
2. In process observing, be as specific as possible in noting what
   people say. Pay close attention to language ("you people," "they,"
   "them"). Also take note of those who support—and show their
   support of—Third World students. Focus on the reactions of the
   participants playing Third World students. Are they realistic? How

[1]This simulation may be substituted for Exercise 11.

do they feel in those roles? Are they self-conscious, overstereo-typing, empathetic?
3. Be sure to leave ample time to process so that participants are not left "hanging" with their feelings.

Time   1 hour (5 minutes for group meetings, 40 minutes for simulation, 15 minutes for processing)

Simulation Design 1: College Setting

The setting is an all-White dormitory. It is late spring, near the end of term. The head of residence will be staying on the next year, and all the counselors for the next year have been chosen. **Situation**

The dorm has a stated commitment to deal with racism. A group of Third World students have been approached by the head of residence to discuss the possibility that some Third World students might move into the dorm. To date no official meetings have taken place to put this into effect. You will all meet to discuss the issues involved.

HEAD OF RESIDENCE **Roles**

You are a White head of residence who has worked hard in your dorm to combat racism. Now there is support from some students to have Third World people move into the dorm. You have been in touch with the Third World student representatives and have some knowledge of their needs. In your position you have the responsibility to meet with the students in your dorm, the counselors, and the Third World students to make sure that any actions taken are productive for all concerned.

COUNSELORS (FOUR)

You are members of an all-White staff in an all-White dorm. As a staff you have stated your agreement with the dorm goals of combating racism. Some residents of your floors are concerned about the possibility of a group of Third World students moving into the dorm. None of you is yet certain how this will affect your own floor, if at all. To date you are not sure what needs and concerns the Third World students have. You are to meet as a group to discuss the issue.

WHITE STUDENTS A (TWO)

You have taken a sociology course on race relations. You are concerned about not having a full educational experience because you live in an all-White dorm. You represent an ad hoc group of students who formed when they heard that a large number of Third World students might move into the dorm.

WHITE STUDENTS B (TWO)

You represent a group of seniors who have lived in the dorm for four years. You are concerned about a number of Third World students moving into the dorm. You are afraid that these students might use dorm dues in an inequitable way and are also concerned about changing the all-White makeup of the dorm. You feel that there is no need for special treatment of Third World students and that, if they want to live in the dorm, they can follow the usual housing procedures.

THIRD WORLD STUDENTS (FOUR)

A number of Third World students have agreed to move into the dorm, providing their needs and concerns can be met. You represent these students and their concerns, which include the following:
1. Dorm activities must be geared to Third World students' needs. You feel that this can best be accomplished by allocating a specific proportion of dorm dues to Third World students who will be living in the dorm and letting you decide how to spend the money for the activities you want.
2. All Third World students want to live together rather than being dispersed throughout the dorm. You also want a Third World counselor on the floor.
3. You want equal representation on the dorm council in order to play an active role in policymaking for the dorm.
4. You do not want to be exploited for White students' learning.

Simulation Design 2: Public School Setting

Nathaniel Hawthorne Middle School is a predominantly White pub- **Situation**
lic school. Of the seven hundred students, seventy-five are Black and
Native American.

Recently there was an incident between two students. A White
male called a Black male "nigger," and a fight ensued. This incident
stirred up many feelings among the Black and Native American
students. They put together a list of demands to present to the administration. At the request of the Third World students the principal has called a meeting with representatives of the Third World
students, counselors, teachers, and White students to discuss the
issues.

PRINCIPAL   **Roles**

You are a White principal, aged forty-five. As principal of Nathaniel
Hawthorne school for the past ten years you have established rapport
with your staff and students. You have a reputation for being sensitive
and fair to all students in your school. You are extremely concerned
about this incident and a bit astonished that racial issues exist in the
school. You had never seen a problem in the school since so few
minority students attended it.

As principal you have the responsibility of calling a meeting with
the representatives of counselors, teachers, and students. Your goal
is to make sure that the actions taken are productive for all concerned
and in the best interests of the school.

COUNSELOR

You are a White counselor who has been at Nathaniel Hawthorne
School for seven years. Your major responsibility is maintenance of
students' records and administration of IQ tests. You believe that IQ
tests are important indicators of students' success in the academic
system.

COUNSELOR

You are a White counselor who has been at Nathaniel Hawthorne School for two and a half years. You have a real concern for the kids at the school and seem to be well liked. In your role you see yourself as really trying to help kids, and many come to you with their personal problems.

TEACHER

You are a White teacher. You were very active in the Civil Rights Movement; in fact, you took part in the Selma march with Dr. King. You strongly believe that people are people.

TEACHER

You are a White teacher. You have strong Christian beliefs. Your basic philosophy has been to turn the other cheek whenever conflict occurs. Your religious philosophy says that all are part of the "brotherhood of man."

TEACHER

You are a White teacher. You have taught at Nathaniel Hawthorne School for twenty years. In fact, the parents of some of the students now in your classes were students of yours.

TEACHER

You are a White teacher. This is your first year at Nathaniel Hawthorne School.

WHITE STUDENT A

You are really concerned about the racial incident and the unrest in the school. You represent an ad hoc group who formed when you heard about the incident. Some of your friends are Black, and they socialize with you. Your group formed to support the Third World group.

WHITE STUDENT B

You are one of a group of White students who banded together when you heard about the incident. You are a friend of the White who was involved and you are very angry about the whole situation. You feel that minorities are just too sensitive and need to realize that the kid didn't mean any harm by his name-calling.

68

THIRD WORLD STUDENTS (TWO)

The incident between the White and Black kids was the straw that broke the camel's back. As a result of the incident you have worked out a list of demands to the school that are *nonnegotiable*. You will not be coerced or co-opted. You have legal connections and if necessary will sue the school for cruel and abusive treatment, as well as for failure to get what you need in the way of an education.

Your grievances and demands include the following:

1. You are tired of the attitudes in school. You are tired of being humiliated, insulted daily by name-calling teachers and students, overt and covert, ("nigger," "colored," "Negro," "savage").
2. You want an end to the all-White curriculum and all-White textbooks. The history taught is only White history. There must be more to history than Blacks as slaves or Native Americans as savages. You are tired of tokenism, such as Black History Week. No Native American history is taught. Is Native American history nonexistent? In literature classes the only novels read are White novels.
3. You refuse to take any more IQ tests. You feel that they are discriminatory and should not be given at all. You are calling for an end to all IQ testing in the school.
4. The school is to do away with the Pledge of Allegiance to the Flag in the mornings until there is freedom and justice for all.
5. Thanksgiving Day should be made a day of mourning. The birthdays of Martin Luther King, Jr., and Malcolm X should be days off.
6. You want Black and Native American teachers and counselors. You feel that the White teachers and counselors are not meeting your needs. Teachers' expectations and attitudes toward you are negative. Counselors merely push you into sports and nonacademic areas.
7. You are tired of being exploited for White students' learning. Whenever an issue involving Blacks or Native Americans comes up, you are asked to tell Whites what it's like to be Black or Native American. Otherwise you are invisible.
8. You want an equal number of representatives on the student council. The total number of representatives is twelve. You want six Third World representatives.

Exercise 13   "The Drawbridge"[1]

Goals   1. To explore individual values connected with institutional racism.
2. To better understand the role of individuals and institutions in racism.

Materials needed   Story "The Drawbridge" (page 72)
Newsprint
Felt markers
Masking tape

Instructions   1. Read to the group the story "The Drawbridge."
2. Ask participants to rank the characters in descending order of responsibility for the death of the baroness (1—most responsible; 6—least responsible). This list should be prepared by one's own value system, not the values of the time of the story.
3. Divide the group into small groups of four to six persons. Have each person share his or her list. Then ask the group to develop a final list by coming to a consensus.
4. Ask each group to report out the final list, giving reasons for the choices. Record each list on newsprint.
5. Then share an alternative way of looking at each character as a symbol of some aspect of modern society:

   Baron = white society.
   Baroness = Third World people and women.
   Gateman = Police force or military.
   Boatman = Institutions.
   Friend = Liberals.
   Lover = Enticements (such as Declaration of Independence, the United States Constitution, other American ideals of freedom)

---

[1]This exercise was developed by Sgt. Charles Howard, Fort Lee, Virginia.

6. Discuss whether this view of the characters in the story influences people to change their lists. Discuss the issues of power, blaming the victim, and action and inaction.

Note to facilitator

1. Give the groups ample time to develop and negotiate their group lists.
2. Depending upon the results in each group, you may want to compare and contrast the assumptions made in each group.
3. Check to see whether the participants' responses change after they see the analogies to modern societal roles. Ask: How often do we look at events as individual incidents outside the societal context? How does that view change the focus and the reality? How often do we blame the victims for attempting to gain something that rightfully belongs to them?

35 to 45 minutes   **Time**

The Drawbridge

As he left for a visit to his outlying districts, the jealous baron warned his pretty wife: "Do not leave the castle while I am gone, or I will punish you severely when I return!"

But as the hours passed, the young baroness grew lonely, and despite her husband's warning she decided to visit her lover, who lived in the countryside nearby.

The castle was situated on an island in a wide, fast-flowing river. A drawbridge linked the island to the mainland at the narrowest point in the river.

"Surely my husband will not return before dawn," she thought, and ordered her servants to lower the drawbridge and leave it down until she returned.

After spending several pleasant hours with her lover, the baroness returned to the drawbridge, only to find it blocked by a gateman wildly waving a long, cruel knife.

"Do not attempt to cross this bridge, Baroness, or I will have to kill you," he cried. "The baron ordered me to do so."

Fearing for her life, the baroness returned to her lover and asked him for help.

"Our relationship is only a romantic one," he said. "I will not help."

The baroness then sought out a boatman on the river, explained her plight to him, and asked him to take her across the river in his boat.

"I will do it, but only if you can pay my fee of five marks."

"But I have no money with me!" the baroness protested.

"That is too bad. No money, no ride," the boatman said flatly.

Her fear growing, the baroness ran crying to the home of a friend and, after explaining her desperate situation, begged for enough money to pay the boatman his fee.

"If you had not disobeyed your husband, this would not have happened," the friend said. "I will give you no money."

With dawn approaching and her last resource exhausted, the baroness returned to the bridge in desperation, attempted to cross to the castle, and was slain by the gateman.

72

Exercise 14   *Black History: Lost, Stolen, or Strayed*

1. To expose participants to institutional racism in education, history, and the communications media.
2. To present some facts to reeducate participants about racism.

Goals

Film *Black History: Lost, Stolen, or Strayed* (Bill Cosby) (page 197)
16-mm movie projector
Screen

**Materials
needed**

1. Show the film *Black History: Lost, Stolen, or Strayed.*
2. Ask participants to share their feelings about the film through "I learned . . ." statements (tell them that they may pass if they do not want to participate).
3. Discuss other reactions to the film:
   a. What did you like or dislike about the film? Why?
   b. As depicted in the film, who is the victim? The victimizer? Did you identify with either one?

Instructions

1. Many participants get "stuck" on the last scene in the film, which shows the Freedom School, and see it as brainwashing. This can lead to an enlightening discussion of how we have been brainwashed in the school systems as they presently operate, including the daily pledge to the flag and other classroom rituals. After this discussion you may want to return to the issue of the Freedom School and look at the necessity for it under present conditions.
2. Go over in detail the segment of the film that deals with education and curriculum. Student participants may say that they have taken Black history courses or that Black history was a part of some other curriculum. It is important to get them to look at whether all aspects of their education incorporate the contributions of all Third World people—especially the courses in which they are currently enrolled. Point out in particular how not American his-

**Note to
facilitator**

73

tory but rather White man's American history is usually taught.

3. You may also discuss the kinds of stereotyping that foster racism, as shown in the segments of the film on the media. How is racism presently acted out in the media (television, movies, commercials)?

4. Many participants may be overwhelmed by this film, for it presents some startling new perspectives and data. It is important to provide time for everyone to share feelings and reactions.

5. It is often very effective to show the first half of the film (ending with the scene from *Guess Who's Coming to Dinner?*), process reactions, and then show the last half of the film. The first half discusses institutional racism in history, music, art, and the media. The second half explores the impact specifically on the Black community.

Time   1½ hours

Exercise 15   The Web of Institutional Racism[1]

Goals

1. To identify various parts of an institution that support racism.
2. To look at practices, policies, and structures that support racism in an institution.
3. To look at interconnections of parts of an institution that make a web reinforcing the power of Whites over Third World people.

Materials needed

Newsprint
Felt markers
Masking tape

Instructions

1. Ask the group to brainstorm the parts of an institution, using an institution with which the participants are familiar.
2. Ask how each part interacts with the others. Does and can any part stand alone? Draw lines to indicate that each part interacts with others. Example:

The Web of Institutional Racism—University Setting

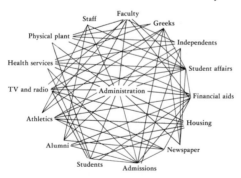

More arrows can be drawn to indicate further interaction of the parts.

[1]Adapted from an exercise developed by Sally Timmel in *White on White: A Handbook for Groups Working Against Racism*, p. 26.

75

3. Discuss practices, policies, and structures within the institution.
   a. Who decides on policies?
   b. Who controls the policies?
   c. For whose needs are the policies, practices, and structures geared?
   d. What kind of controls do Third World people have in the system?

Note to facilitator

1. It is important to discuss how institutions are created to meet people's needs. Explore how and if the institutions meet those needs. Again, it is vital to touch on the issues of power and control within the system. Who sets policies and practices? How does one gain access to power positions within the system?
2. It is also crucial to deal with the inconsistencies. What is the institutional attitude, and what is the actual behavior? How do the policies and/or practices facilitate or inhibit actualizing the attitudes in the system?
3. It is essential for the facilitator to have some working knowledge of the system that the group is exploring.

Time 35 to 45 minutes

Exercise 16   The Effects of Institutional Racism on Native Americans

1. To expose participants to the effects of institutional racism on Native Americans.
2. To hear about these effects in a Native American's words.
3. To highlight basic inconsistencies in American heritage and behavior.

Goals

Tape or record *The Best of Buffy Saint Marie* (selections "Now That the Buffalo's Gone," "My Country 'Tis of Thee—Your People are Dying") (page 197)
Cassette or record player

Materials needed

1. Play the two selections listed above.
2. Ask participants to share their reactions.
3. Discuss the following:
   a. The smallpox–blankets–for–land form of genocide.
   b. Manifest destiny—an excuse for genocide.
   c. The stereotypes of Native Americans.
   d. Reservations today—who has the power and control?
4. Discuss the inconsistencies of "American heritage and culture" and the treatment of Native Americans.
5. Discuss how institutional racism camouflages the real actions of White Americans, as well as disregarding the contributions of Third World people to American society.

Instructions

These selections highlight issues of racism and genocide against Native Americans and expose participants to some of the inconsistencies and hypocrisies in America's present and past. This exercise can also focus on the functioning of institutional racism in education as revealed by what is included in curriculum and textbooks and what is left out. The media stereotypes of Native Americans in film—programs and commercials—can also be explored.

Note to facilitator

30 to 45 minutes

Time

Exercise 17   Debate[1]

Goals   1. To have participants discuss an issue involving racism in a debate format.
2. To try to "stretch" participants' attitudes by encouraging them to look at both sides of an issue.

Materials needed   None

Instructions   1. Choose an issue that you feel the group is interested in working on or needs to work on. Examples:
   a. Racism as the responsibility of White people.
   b. The power of the White people in this group to combat racism.
   c. Busing—integration of schools.
   d. Affirmative Action—is it facilitating the demise of institutional racism?
2. Form the group as follows: three judges, one timekeeper, a pro side, and a con side.
3. Give each side (pro and con) ten minutes to prepare arguments. Then divide the time as follows:

   Three-minute opening statement (pro and con)
   Two-minute break
   Two-minute rebuttal (pro and con)
   Five-minute open discussion
   One-minute summary (pro and con)

4. The judges then take five minutes to decide the winner of the debate. This decision is based on the way the arguments are presented. Share the decision with the group.

---

[1]This exercise is optional. It should be used if time permits and/or the climate in the group makes it seem appropriate.

You may want to discuss how the participants felt taking the sides to their actual beliefs.they took, especially if the arguments they supported were contrary **Note to**
to their actual beliefs. **facilitator**

35 to 40 minutes **Time**

Exercise 18   Some Perspectives on Institutional Racism

Goals   1. To explore and clarify the effects of institutional racism on Black people.
2. To be exposed to a Black perspective on racism.
3. To examine further the inconsistencies between the White society's ideology and its behavior.

Materials needed   Tape or record *The Light Side: The Dark Side* (Dick Gregory) (page 197)
Cassette or record player

Instructions   1. You may choose to play any or all of the following selections, depending on where the group is and the amount of time available or desirable. The following selections are recommended:
   a. "White Racist Institutions and Black Rioters," side 3 (15 min. 35 sec.). This selection gives an overview of White racism and White people's role and responsibility in it. It highlights inconsistencies in White American ideology as exemplified in the Declaration of Independence. This selection is indispensable to the goals of this stage.
   b. "American History," side 3 (4 min. 30 sec.). This selection looks at "American" history and shows how it is really White history. It raises questions about who writes history books and the meaning of IQ tests.
   c. "Property Rights—Human Rights," side 2 (11 min. 35 sec.). Here Gregory discusses basic American values. The selection is helpful in revealing inconsistencies in priorities and attitudes prevalent in White American society.
2. Discuss reactions to the selections.

This exercise helps clarify White people's responsibility for racism in America. The record selections are confronting. They are blunt and to the point, and the arguments are presented in such a way that they are hard for participants to refute. The record is thus a powerful tool. It should be presented at a time when tension in the group is high.

30 to 45 minutes

Exercise 19   In-Depth Exploration of Institutional
                Racism in Specific Institutions: Projects[1]

Goals   To help participants begin to identify for themselves the ways in
         which institutional racism functions.

Materials   Newsprint
needed   Felt markers
          Masking tape
          "Inventory of Racism" (page 83)

Instructions   1. Form small groups of four to six persons.
                2. Brainstorm a list of various institutions in American society—
                   business, educational, religious, and governmental institutions.
                3. Ask each group to choose one institution and as a group project
                   examine how racism functions in it overtly and covertly. The
                   "Inventory of Racism" will be helpful in this process.
                4. Have the groups report out. The time for reporting out depends on
                   the format of the group—whether it is a long-term course or a
                   short workshop. The project can be completed during a lunch
                   period or a day or two later.

Note to   1. In this exercise participants begin to examine institutional racism
facilitator   on their own, as well as gain insight into the dynamics of racism.
               2. If preferred, the groups may report out at the conclusion of Exer-
                  cise 20.

Time   10 minutes to set up groups, 5 to 10 minutes report-out time per
        group

[1]This exercise is optional for this stage. It should be used if time permits. Exercise
20 may be substituted for it.

Inventory of Racism

How to Look for Institutional Racism[2]

I. Employment:

What percentage of workers are black? white? male? female? at each job level?

How are employees recruited? Does company have stated policy regarding equal employment opportunity? What is it? Is it publicized within the company? in the community? Is an employment agency used? Where are openings announced? Are openings announced to current employees only? Are openings in higher levels made known to present employees? Are jobs advertised in news media? in black community news media? What is turnover? black? white? Does the company use or have an employment center in the ghetto? Is there an aggressive policy—visiting high schools, scholarships, and job promises made to students in high schools and colleges if students engage in particular programs?

What kind of application is used? Does it contain discriminatory and/or unnecessary questions?

Who does the interviewing? black or white persons? What training does the personnel director have in dealing with and understanding different peoples?

What are the criteria for different jobs? Are they objectively and consistently used? Are they written down? Can they be written down? If not, why not?

What are salaries at each job level? Are they uniform among employees at each level?

[2]Committee for One Society [Chicago], "Inventory of Racism: How to Look for Institutional Racism"; reproduced in Robert E. Terry, *For Whites Only* (Grand Rapids, Mich., Wm. B. Eerdsmans, 1970), pp. 101–104. Used by permission.

How are people promoted within the company? Are there mechanisms set up to train for promotion? Who get information about promotion? Is promotion a possibility for all employees? Is promotion a formal process, or is it the result of social contacts? Who ride together to work? Who eat lunch together? Do employees belong to social clubs, etc., outside of company where company business gets done? What kind of special coaching and counseling is provided? Is special counseling provided to help black employees face problems of competition with more aggressive and prejudiced white employees? Is company and/or union newspaper used to announce new jobs, programs, promotions? What kinds of images are projected in newspaper? Who writes it? art work? Who prints it? Is information about training opportunities, etc., put up on company bulletin board?

What kinds of facilities are there for workers? recreational clubs? teams? Where do they play? Where are company picnics held? Who come?

Who makes final decisions on hiring and upgrading?

Are tests used to screen job applicants? Are tests equitable for blacks and whites? in results? What are patterns of test scores for different groups? Who made up tests? Have they been locally validated? Who administers tests? Who scores tests? Are employees tested on the job, e.g., using the machine they will be hired to operate? Are all applicants tested on the same machine? Do tests examine qualified or qualifiables? Is there on-the-job training? for whom? How are people recruited for it? Who runs training? Are supervisors trained to be sensitive to minority workers? What types of jobs are people trained for? Are jobs marginal or subject to elimination by automation?

What are employment benefits? Do all workers receive them? Is it policy to acquaint all employees with health insurance programs, for example? Do executives get stock options? social club memberships?

Is entry possible at all levels, or must everyone come up through the ranks?

II. Are black suppliers and services used?
scavengers?
exterminators?
janitorial services?
office supplies?
accounting?
lawyers? doctors?
contractors?
answering service?
window washing?
banking? (including mortgages and loans)
insurances?
food products? (milk, orange juice, etc.)
maintenance supplies? (wax, bleach, etc.)

III. Investments:
What property is owned? Is property rented? for how much?

What are policies of firms renting in areas here discussed? Other investments?

Who handles portfolio? through what bank or finance company?

Who owns stock in company? in what amounts? Who are stockholders. Where do they live?

What are the policies of the companies in which investments are made—in areas under consideration here? employment? use of black services, etc.?

What are policies of white suppliers in areas considered here?

IV. Advertising:
What company is employed? kind of contract? size of account?

Models employed? images projected? of product? company? society?

Where is advertising done? what media used? in what communities?

Who does public relations work? Where is work done?

85

How important is advertising? What proportion of business is invested there?

Whom is advertising aimed at?

Are black images projected in black media or in all media?

What are policies in employment, use of black services, etc.?

All supplies of services and materials should be examined in a similar way?

What does the primary company under examination do to influence policies of suppliers?

V. Government:
Is federal government involved in business or program? through what agency locally? How was it obtained? How is it used?

Does institution receive special consideration from government locally?

Who is alderman, congressman, etc.? Who represents area institution is based in?

Does institution depend on "good" relationship with public officials? Who?

VI. Board of directors and others:
Who is on board of directors? Who are officers?

What other boards do they sit on?

What social clubs do members belong to? voluntary associations?

What do members get paid per meeting?

Do members own significant portion of stock in company?

What other companies do members own stock in?

Do directors receive special stock options? What are they?

How does one get on the board? How long do they sit on it?

Is board important in setting policy or only rubber stamp?

Where do members live?

What are important social contacts and relationships with other influential people?

VII. Merchandising/Retail:
Percentage of credit accounts in white community? black community?

How are credit ratings obtained? Who processes them?

How does institution operate—through mail? phone? over the counter?

Do people subscribe to receive product? to receive information?

Are blacks involved in granting credit?

VIII. Unions:
Does institution hire union employees? Is union discriminatory?

Is recruitment through union?

Apprenticeships available? for whom?

How does union bank? Who runs union?

(Same questions apply to a union as to an institution in general)

How does the union relate to the black community?

Does the union have black stewards? black officers?

IX. What contributions are made to the community by companies and officers?

Contributions to the Joint Negro College Fund?

Programs to help house employees in presently segregated areas?

Contributions to NAACP Legal Defense Fund, community organizations in black communities, Urban League, etc.?

Use of money and power in issues crucial to the black community?

X. Is there a company committee to develop and carry out a program for implementation of a nonracist policy?
(a) Company officers appointed to supervise a program
(b) Regular examinations of compliance with policies

(c) Education of all levels of management

(d) Persons appointed to relate especially to black services and suppliers

XI. What image is created by company?
Contents of bulletin boards?
Menus in restaurants?
Pictures on the walls?

Exercise 20	More Perspectives on Institutional Racism[1]

1. To explore the role of economics in institutional racism. 2. To explore White American history and racism and its effects in the development of the United States.	**Goals**

Tape or record *Chastisement* (The Last Poets), (selections "Before the White Man Came," E Pluribus Unum") (page 198) Cassette or record player	**Materials needed**

1. Play "Before the White Man Came" (the selection may also be helpful if used after Exercise 16 or, in Stage 4, after Exercise 30). It is useful for participants to have access to the lyrics. 2. Discuss the effects of White settlement on Native Americans. Discuss reactions to the selection. 3. Play "E Pluribus Unum." Again, access to the lyrics is helpful. 4. Discuss the effects of economics on racism and Third World people. The discussion of economics can range from the beginning of the institution of slavery to the present. Discuss personal reactions to the selection.	**Instructions**

1. These selections seem to be threatening to participants. To some Whites the Last Poets come off as extremely angry and/or militant. Many White participants may have trouble dealing with their style. It thus serves as a good confrontation tool. 2. This exercise can also be used in Stage 4. At that time discuss the cultural aspects—music, style, and content—in dealing with cultural values.	**Note to facilitator**

30 minutes	**Time**

[1]This exercise is optional. It should be used if time permits. It may be substituted for Exercise 18.

Exercise 21   Reality Testing: How Much Have I Been
               Cheated in My Education?[1]

Goals   To help participants see how much has been omitted from their edu-
           cation as a result of institutional racism.

Materials Daniels Interracial Apperception and Ideology Test (page 198)
needed   Black History Test (page 198)

Instructions 1. Administer either of the above tests.
              2. Grade the tests as a group.
              3. Discuss the participants' reactions to taking the test and their
                 scores.
                 a. Discuss how they felt knowing or not knowing the answers.
                 b. Discuss what their scores indicate about institutional racism
                    in education.
              4. Compare the test with standardized IQ tests and the probable
                 effects of such tests on Third World people.

Note to   1. This exercise helps participants get in touch with feelings of frus-
facilitator   tration. Most of them will be unfamiliar with the material present-
              ed in the tests. They will react with some anxiety. It is helpful to
              discuss how Third World people must feel when they take IQ tests.
              Emphasize that the people and their contributions named in the
              test are just as important as White leaders and their achievements
              but that they are not generally known to Whites. This leads into
              a deeper exploration of institutional racism in education.

[1]This exercise is optional. It should be used if time permits.

2. You may want to administer this test at the beginning of Stage 2 to emphasize the need to look at institutional racism.

1 hour (30 minutes to administer, 30 minutes to grade and discuss)   **Time**

Stage 3   Dealing with Feelings

Exercise 22   The Here-and-Now Wheel   page   97

23   Fears of Dealing with Racism   98

24   The Circle Break-in   100

25   Fantasy   102
        "Fantasy: Bus Trip"   103
        "Whose Fantasy? or, Do I Know Reality
            When I See It?"   104

26   Personal Racial Experience   105
        Inventory of Racial Experience   106

See Appendix, pages 188 and 197, for readings and resources for Stage 2.

Stage 3   Dealing with Feelings

In Stages 1 and 2 participants explored racism on an intellectual level by dealing with specific kinds of racism. This approach may seem somewhat removed from participants' own lives. Many feelings were experienced during those two stages, however, and those feelings form the basis for the next stage. Stage 3 shifts to a more personal dimension by exploring what is happening inside participants as a result of the materials presented in the first two stages. The exercises in Stage 3 are designed to:

1. Support participants' sharing of personal feelings produced by the experiences of Stages 1 and 2.
2. Help them get in touch with their fears of and fantasies about Third World people.
3. Facilitate their sorting through their feelings.
4. Help them become open about their feelings so that they can continue their exploration of racism on a more personal level in Stages 4 to 6.

In Stages 1 and 2 most participants were exposed to many new ideas and perspectives. Constantly bombarded with sometimes shocking new information, they have many questions and feelings. In some these questions begin to cause inner conflicts. On the one hand, for a number of years they have believed and thought one way; now they begin to see that what they have been taught or what they have believed may not be true or accurate (Columbus did not really *discover* America!). Conflicts and doubt arise. Their "truths" are being called into question.

Stage 3 is a crucial stage in the process of reeducating White people. It is not enough to deal with racism solely on a cognitive level. If participants are not touched personally—if their emotional base does not change at this point—they are unlikely to change their attitudes and behaviors. If participants see racism only from an intellectual perspective, the impact on their attitudes is slight and

93

will not produce any significant change in their behavior. If, however, they are internally moved and emotionally involved in dealing with and understanding racism, there is a much greater possibility that their behavior too will change. They will have a personal investment—a stake—in the issue.

Stages 1 and 2 help raise participants' consciousness of what White racism is and how it functions. Many people enter Stage 3 sitting on a host of feelings, overwhelmed by the new data, confused about what is really the "truth," and/or helpless about what to do with it all. Other people may be feeling guilty about being racist or being White. Some may feel a responsibility for racism because they are White or angry about the way the system has treated Third World people. In Stage 2 many of these feelings must be brought out and dealt with; otherwise they will begin to immobilize the participants and stifle growth in any positive direction. The exercises in Stage 3 help participants get in touch with their "here-and-now" feelings, deal with them, and move into a process of change and growth.

Stage 3 is also concerned with helping participants explore their unconscious feelings. Feelings at the unconscious level include fears and fantasies related to racism. These fears and fantasies are a result of personal experiences, as well as stereotypes and myths about Third World people with which they have been indoctrinated. Several of the exercises in Stage 3 are designed to draw out these fantasies and fears and help participants sort through them.

The main objective of Stage 3, therefore, is to facilitate participants' discussion of their feelings, to help them not only share those feelings but also sort through and integrate them so that they will be able to move into the succeeding stages.

Method Unlike Stages 1 and 2, which were primarily content-oriented, Stage 3 is focused on process issues. The success of this stage therefore depends largely upon the facilitator's "human relations" skills—that is, her or his ability to help participants reveal their feelings, fears, and fantasies about racism, examine those feelings, and evaluate them. The supportive climate that has developed through Stages 1 and 2 will give participants a sense of commonality and trust. If they can sense the support of the group, they will not feel alone with their feelings.

In this stage the facilitator again has a dual function: to be sup-

94

porting of participants but also firm in presenting alternative perspectives. For example: Someone in the group is telling about once having been robbed by a Black person. Now the participant experiences fear of being robbed whenever he or she sees a Black person. To support that fear would only be supporting the person's racism. The role of the facilitator may be to acknowledge that being robbed might well be a frightening experience but also to ask whether, if the robber had been White, the person would be afraid of being robbed whenever he or she saw a White person. It is necessary to probe why the person generalizes about a race from one incident involving one individual and how one incident can thus support one's racism. In presenting an alternate perspective, the facilitator must also help participants explore the myths and attempt to break through some of the stereotyping. If participants express feelings of helplessness, the facilitator must offer the alternative of action—to assure them that there are positive steps that they can take. Feelings of helplessness and guilt immobilize people. The facilitator must manage to give support and at the same time facilitate participants' exploration and integration of their feelings. To move the group through this stage successfully requires a good deal of skill.

The exercises for this stage have been developed as starting points that will probe the participants' deeper personal feelings—the real ones. They are tools to facilitate further probing of attitudes.[1] The sorting-out process does not end with Stage 3, however. Participants should be encouraged to continue to work through their feelings during the remainder of the training program, outside the group, and after the program has ended.

Stage 3 is an indicator of how well the goals of Stages 1 and 2 have been met. If in Stage 3 participants display some confusion and appear to be caught up in their feelings, you know that you are probably getting through to them. The more their inner emotions are involved and explored the greater the likelihood that they will be willing—even eager—to take action to combat racism.

[1]An alternative approach for this stage is to use a combination of the unstructured T-group format with Exercise 25, "Fantasy."

Exercise 22   The Here-and-Now Wheel

1. To bring to the surface feelings that evolved in Stages 1 and 2.   **Goals**
2. To determine participants' feeling levels.
3. To provide a structured mechanism for beginning to explore feelings.

Paper   **Materials**
Pens or pencils   **needed**

1. Ask participants to draw a circle and divide it into quarters.   **Instructions**
2. Ask them to write in each quarter one feeling that they have *"right now,"* as a result of the workshop so far.
3. Ask them to share their lists with the group or, alternatively, to share their lists in pairs or small groups.

1. The facilitator's role is to help draw out participants' feelings and   **Note to**
   try to gain support in the group for each individual's feeling level.   **facilitator**
   The climate should be such that participants will offer their reactions and support to one another.
2. Have the participants try to clarify where their feelings are coming from—that is, identify the exercises or group experiences that produced the feelings.

Varies, depending on the issues in the group   **Time**

Exercise 23   Fears of Dealing with Racism

Goals   1. To have participants get in touch with fears centering on dealing with racism.
2. To help them express fears directly involving racism.
3. To help them explore myths and stereotypes connected with their fears.
4. To help them explore personal experiences connected with those fears.

Materials needed   Paper
Pens or pencils

Instructions   1. Ask participants to list five fears that they have about dealing with their racism. When they have completed the list, ask them to write down five fears they have that are connected to racism—a stereotype, a personal experience, a myth, and so on.
2. Ask participants to share their five fears. Continue with the second list.

Note to facilitator   1. There are two parts to this exercise. The first deals with fears of confronting racism that may be operating in the group. It also looks at reasons why people may be holding in their feelings or blocking themselves from looking at their own behavior. Typical responses are: "I fear discovering that I'm unalterably racist"; "I fear being misunderstood if I start to think out loud in the group"; "I fear that perhaps I am more racist than I thought I was"; "I fear that I won't have the guts, or caring, to do something about it"; "I fear realizing my ignorance." All these fears indicate some kind of block in the group. The facilitator must help participants not only name their fears but also explore them. It may be helpful to ask the question, "What is the worst thing that could happen to you if your fear came true?" This activity allows participants to get in touch with the limits and boundaries of their fears.

2. The second part of the exercise is designed to help participants examine their internal fears connected with racism. These include attitudes built on personal experiences, as well as stereotypes and myths. It is important first to determine which category the fear is based on. If it is built on myths, for example, it may be helpful to discuss where the myths came from historically and how as a result racism has been deeply ingrained in all of us. If the fear developed out of a personal experience, it is important to look at the process of generalizing from one incident and see how such generalizing also perpetuates racism. The question should be asked, "Would a White feel the same toward all other Whites if there had been a similar experience with a White person?"

3. It is also important to discuss how we tend to fear what we do not know or understand. When we encounter people with a different life-style from our own, we sometimes reject them out of ignorance or because their "difference" seems threatening. Oftentimes that is the source of our fears.

4. This exercise facilitates participants' in-depth examination of internal feelings centering on racism.

Varies, depending upon the issues in the group   **Time**

Exercise 24   The Circle Break-in

Goals   1. To have participants get in touch with their feelings of power.
2. To have participants get in touch with their power as White people to exclude Third World people.
3. To have participants experience how it feels to be excluded.
4. To explore individual feelings about this power as they relate to racism.

Materials needed   None

Instructions   1. Ask the participants to form a circle.
2. Ask them to begin thinking about how they feel within that circle —being aware of who is in it and looking at and observing one another.
3. Ask that one person volunteer to step outside the circle.
4. Tell the person that the group has something that he or she wants. The person must find a way into the circle.
5. Tell the group members that they are to find ways to keep the person out.
6. While the outsider is trying to get in, the facilitator should process what is occurring.
7. After the outsider has reentered the group, ask for a second volunteer. Repeat this procedure until everyone has been outside the circle.
8. Process the exercise:
    a. How did participants feel outside the circle?
    b. How did they feel if they got in?
    c. What mechanisms or tactics did they use to get in?
    d. Why did they try to get in—that is, what did the group have that they wanted?
    e. How did they feel being a part of the circle while others were trying to get in?

f. How can this exercise be related to racism?

g. If they managed to get in, what made them feel a part of the group?

This exercise helps participants explore their own feelings about racism by drawing out their own power and helping them get in touch with it. The whole question of exclusion and fighting for one's rights can be considered. The exercise demonstrates how people may be supporting racism unintentionally without being actively racist.

Note to facilitator

45 minutes to 1 hour

Time

101

Exercise 25   Fantasy

Goals   To have participants get in touch with their fears and fantasies relating to racism.

Materials needed   "Fantasy: Bus Trip" (page 102) or
"Whose Fantasy? or, Do I Know Reality When I See It?" (page 104)

Instructions   1. Ask participants to find a convenient place in the room and lie down in a comfortable position. Ask them to close their eyes and relax (you may want to do a relaxation exercise before beginning the fantasy).
2. Read aloud one of the fantasies. Ask the participants to imagine the scene and fill in the blanks in their minds. Tell them to note in their minds and bodies their reactions, feelings, and thoughts.
3. Ask them to share their fantasies with the group. Have each person finish before going on to the next person.
4. Discuss the meaning and implications of each person's fantasy.

Note to facilitator   1. It is extremely important that participants do not compare their fantasies. Each person's fantasy relates to her or his own personal feelings and reactions. Participants who begin to compare or evaluate others' fantasies should be stopped.
2. This exercise is a catalyst in the probing of White people's myths and stereotypes relating to Third World people. It can be a very deep experience, touching upon some strong feelings and fears. Time should be allotted so that all members of the group can share their fantasies, if they choose to do so, and the results can be adequately processed.

Time   Varies, depending upon the number in the group and the openness of the participants

Fantasy: Bus Trip

You are taking a transcontinental bus to New York City. It is your first trip to New York. The ride has been quite pleasurable. . . . It is a warm summer evening. . . . You feel . . ..

You look around the bus and notice that all the passengers on the bus are White. . . . You feel . . ..

The trip is coming to a close. You are approaching New York. . . . You notice . . .. You feel . . ..

You are now driving through Harlem. . . . You notice . . .. You feel . . ..

All of a sudden the bus stops. . . . You feel . . ..

The bus driver says that everyone must get out. The bus has broken down. . . . You notice . . .. You feel . . ..

Complete the scene.

Whose Fantasy? or, Do I Know Reality When I See It?

You are driving home alone at night from a meeting. Traveling on a well-lighted freeway running through the center of a large metropolitan area, you see flashing lights ahead. You slow down and note that traffic is being directed off the freeway at a point where temporary repairs are being made. At the end of the exit is a detour sign directing you onto a shabby, ill-lighted, dirty, seemingly deserted street.

It is a hot summer night, and your car is not air-conditioned. You have been driving with all the windows wide open. When you see the detour, you . . ..

As you proceed down the street, you see ahead a group of people gathered near a store on the corner. Some are standing in the street. . . . As you slow down to avoid the people in the street, you see them turn to look at your car. . . .

A man steps out of the group and moves toward your car with his hand raised. . . . He has something in his hand that he is waving. . . . He is also saying something. . . . His expression is . . ..

Then you notice that there seems to be someone lying in the center of the group on the sidewalk. . . . The people in the group have expressions on their faces that seem to be . . ..

At the same time you see, three or four blocks away, flashing lights like those that directed you off the freeway. . . . You feel . . .. You drive . . ..

Exercise 26   Personal Racial Experience

Goals

1. To have participants explicitly record their personal experiences and actions concerning racism.
2. To prepare participants to move into Stage 4.

Materials needed

"Inventory of Racial Experience" (page 106)

Instructions

1. Sometime before the session give out copies of "Inventory of Racial Experience."
2. Ask participants to select from the twelve categories items that are most meaningful to them and to complete the inventory by describing a specific event or experience, including day, place, and circumstance, if possible, for the selected items.
3. Ask participants to share a few of the incidents that are the most meaningful for them.
4. Discuss participants' reactions to completing the inventory.
5. Discuss patterns and similarities in individuals' responses to the inventory.

Note to facilitator

1. Try to focus on feelings connected with the incident instead of allowing the discussion to move into an intellectual one. This can get "heady" unless you probe into why the person remembered or chose a particular incident. Concentrate on asking how it affected him or her and what emotional impact it had.
2. You can also give out a Black version of the inventory so that participants can have an alternate perspective (page 107).

Time

Varies, depending upon the issues in the group

Inventory of Racial Experience[1]

There are two forms of this inventory, one for Whites and one for Blacks. Each form contains roughly parallel questions reflecting two points of view about critical incidents in the development of racial awareness. There are several potential uses for this inventory: to conduct a personal review of one's race-related experiences so that patterns and changes become clearer; to compare your experience with variations in the lives of others of your race; to contrast with the perspectives of people of another race. The basic purpose of the inventory is to elicit the assumptions that guide interpretations of racial events and direct actions concerning race.

For each of the twelve incidents listed, try to think of a specific event or experience—the day, place, and circumstance, if possible. As you review and describe each experience, bear in mind the following questions:

1. When did it occur? How old were you?
2. What happened? What led up to the situation? What did you think, feel, and do?
3. What are you doing now?
4. What will you do?

Completing this inventory may take an hour or more. The detail necessary for adequate answers will depend on the uses to which the inventory is to be put.

Name _____   Date _____

Being White

1. Treating Blacks differently from Whites.
2. Learning that Whites created and maintained slavery.
3. Becoming aware of discrimination against Blacks.
4. Feeling more fortunate than, superior to, or better than Blacks.

---

[1]Developed by Frederick C. Jefferson, University of Rochester.

5. Trying consciously to be especially good, kind, helpful, or loving to Blacks.
6. Desiring to prove that you really are equal to or the same as Blacks.
7. Being angry at other Whites for what they were doing to Blacks.
8. Admiring and wishing that you or Whites were more like Blacks in some specific way(s).
9. Feeling helpless as an individual to do anything truly useful in changing White racism.
10. Deciding to actively resist those social and/or political and/or economic forces that cause feelings of worthlessness in and subjugate Black people.
11. Wanting to get over feelings of guilt and shame about being subconsciously racist.
12. Becoming aware of the need for a spiritual center.

Being Black

1. Discovering that being Black made a difference to others.
2. Learning that Blacks were slaves.
3. Becoming aware of the social position of Blacks in America.
4. Wishing and hoping to be seen as equal to Whites.
5. Desiring to experience acceptance and/or love from a White person.
6. Experiencing the desire to prove how equal and superior you were to Whites.
7. Discovering deep resentment and distrust of other Blacks.
8. Wishing that Black female and/or Black male intimates possessed the positive qualities of their White counterparts.
9. Discovering that a Black community united in purpose can begin to crush obstacles (real and imagined) to Black social, political, economic, and personal growth.
10. Deciding to actively resist those social and/or political and/or economic forces that cause feelings of powerlessness and/or worthlessness in Black people.
11. Becoming aware of the desire to discover your self-power, your personhood, and ways to answer the question, Who am I?
12. Becoming aware of the need for a spiritual center.

Stage 4   Cultural Differences: Exploring Cultural
           Racism

Exercise 27   Language: Cultural Racism Begins
                with Words   page 113

        28   Language: Words Do Matter   115

        29   Cultural Differences: Black Is . . ., White
                Is   117

        30   Language: Cultural Racism at Its Extreme?
                The Klan   119

        31   Mini-Lecture: The Historical Roots of
                Cultural Racism   121

        32   IQ: The Dove Counter Balance Test   124
                The Dove Counter Balance Test   126

        33   IQ: The Shockley-Poussaint Debate   133

See Appendix, pages 191 and 197, for readings and resources for Stage 4.

Stage 4 Cultural Differences: Exploring Cultural Racism

Introduction

The participants have sorted through some of their feelings and made some sense out of them in Stage 3. They continue their exploration of racism in Stage 4. This stage focuses on another level of racism — cultural racism. Here the participants will be introduced to exercises designed to:

1. Help them understand what cultural racism is.
2. Help them become aware of cultural differences between Whites and Third World people.
3. Help them see connections between their own environment and actions that may support cultural racism.

Rationale

So that participants will be ready to confront and examine their personal racism, they must first understand the roots of it. Much of White people's individual and personal racism is developed and supported by cultural racism. Therefore, Stage 4 is a crucial stage in fully understanding one's personal and individual racism. Stage 4 helps participants explore cultural racism — one group's (White people's) domination over another (Third World people) in terms of values, norms, and standards. Stage 4 is concerned with exploring the dominant White American norms and values and their effect on minorities and Whites.

The exercises in this stage examine the values that underlie the "English language," the customs of dress, the holidays of White culture, the standards Whites hold about what is "good" art and music, beauty, and intelligence. Cultural racism is also explored as the basis of many of the myths and stereotypes that White people accept about Third World people, for example, myths about Black people's sexuality and stereotypes about minorities being lazy, dirty, or animalistic. Also examined is the notion of America as a "melting pot" and what that expression really means — that all cultures must become White in their standards and values. It is extremely important that participants begin to realize that cultural racism does exist in America, in that everything is judged by White standards.

109

In this stage participants begin to realize how pervasive cultural racism is, in that it affects institutional values and thereby supports institutional racism, as well as affecting and helping Whites formulate personal values and thereby support their individual racism. The exercises in this stage demonstrate how ingrained this form of racism is—we can hardly escape from it in any aspect of our society. The main point that Stage 4 makes is that the basic functioning of cultural racism is in the use of White standards to judge minorities and their life-styles. Participants begin to realize that the use of White standards by individuals and by the system—as exemplified by college admissions offices, employment agencies, standardized tests—to judge Third World people is cultural racism. They are then one step further in their exploration and understanding of racism.

Part of this understanding develops when participants realize that Third World people often have different perspectives and cultures from those of Whites. Therefore, a second part of this stage explores the reality that cultural differences exist. Gross injustices can occur when Whites assume that there are no differences between members of the different minorities and White people—that is, when Whites say, "People are people," or, "When I see someone who's Black, color is not an issue." Some of the exercises in Stage 2 are also helpful here. Helping participants understand the historical roots of Blacks (Africans) and Whites (Europeans) is a way to help them realize that there are clear differences between Whites and Third World people that must be noted and accepted.

Stage 4 also points out more inconsistencies between American ideology and Americans' behavior. American ideology includes the belief that all people should have the right to life, liberty, and the pursuit of happiness. Pressure on a group of people to conform to the life-style and values of another group of people interferes with that ideology. The present standards and norms, which were set up by Whites, are also inconsistent with that ideology. Stage 4 explores these inconsistencies as another component of the American Dilemma.

Finally, Stage 4 helps participants draw some connections between the norms and values in their own environment and cultural racism. This insight prepares them for Stage 5, in which they will explore their individual racism.

110

Stage 4 presents some different dynamics for the facilitator. When **Method** you are working on the issue of cultural racism, you are drawing somewhat closer to the participants' own values and attitudes. They can become very defensive at this point. On the other hand, by now there should be some acceptance of racism as a White problem and a willingness to learn more about the depth of racism. Moreover, by now the support system within the group should be firm, and the participants should be feeling a commitment to grow and learn together. The facilitator must process more closely personal behaviors and ideologies that seem to grow out of cultural racism. This feedback must be given immediately so that participants can become aware of the ways in which cultural racism affects their individual behavior.

In this stage the facilitator strives for an awareness of the functioning of cultural racism. Participants need to understand that racism is perpetuated when White standards are used to judge Third World people and is built on the assumption that the cultures of Third World people are no different from the White culture. That is essentially the task in Stage 4. The facilitator must see that this task is accomplished, as well as prepare participants to look at their own behavior in Stage 5.

As in the earlier stages, the facilitator needs to be supportive but also firm. The facilitator should keep in mind some of the guidelines stated in the "Method" sections of the first three stages and follow them where appropriate in Stage 4 as well.

Exercise 27   Language: Cultural Racism Begins with Words

1. To help participants recognize how deeply rooted racism is in our system.
2. To help participants recognize how the English language supports racism.

Dictionary (several copies, if possible)
Newsprint
Felt markers
Masking tape

1. Ask a participant to look up the meaning of the word *red* in the dictionary and read it aloud to the group.
2. Write the definition on newsprint.
3. Ask another person to look up the word *yellow* and read the definition aloud. Write the definition on newsprint.
4. Do the same for the words *black* and *white.*
5. Compare and discuss the following:
   a. Definitions associated with the word *white* as compared with *yellow, red,* and *black,* all of which indicate racial colors.
   b. What the different definitions say about the way the White culture sees people of color.
   c. What that says about the values the English language portrays.
   d. Why English is spoken in schools. How that standard oppresses Spanish-speaking people, Native Americans, Asian-Americans, Afro-Americans.

1. Note that most of the words defining *white* have positive connotations. The definitions of *black, yellow,* and *red,* which symbolize Third World people, contain many more negative terms.
2. This exercise can lead to a discussion about why English is the dominant language taught in the schools. Discuss the following:

What effect does this standard have on children of other cultures? Why is Black dialect called "nonstandard" English and a southern dialect is not? Why do many bilingual programs see knowledge of two languages as a deficit and not an asset?

3. Discuss how language demonstrates our view of the world, as well as our underlying values and assumptions.
4. This exercise begins to deal with the notion of America as a melting pot. What is the melting pot? How are people of other cultures supposed to fit into the melting pot, which tries to melt all peoples and shape them into White standards, including White language? Why must all people conform, rather than having the freedom to live according to their own culture and standards? This exercise pinpoints these and other inconsistencies.

Time   25 minutes

Exercise 28   Language: Words Do Matter

1. To continue to explore the power of language in terms of cultural racism.   **Goals**
2. To continue to explore the ways in which the English language is used to support and perpetuate the racist system.

Newsprint   **Materials**
Felt markers   **needed**
Masking tape

1. Ask the participants to make lists of expressions and/or sayings   **Instructions**
   that contain the word *white* ("white knight," "white as snow,"
   "whitewash," and so on). Then brainstorm lists of words and/or
   sayings that contain the word *black* ("black sheep," "blacklist,"
   "black magic," and so on).
2. Compare and contrast the lists.
   a. How many items in the "white" list have positive connotations?
      Negative connotations?
   b. How many items in the "black" list have positive connotations?
      Negative connotations?
3. Discuss cultural values and standards.
   a. What are positive and negative in terms of colors?
   b. How do those values become translated and reflected onto peo-
      ple of that color—that is, that race?
   c. Who sets up standards of "proper" English?
   d. Who has the power to decide what are the norms—for example,
      that English will be taught as the dominant language?
4. Explore other issues:
   a. What are the norms—characteristics—of beauty? Who decides
      them?
   b. Who decides what days the country will celebrate as holidays?
      What do the legal holidays indicate to Third World people?
   c. What are the standards for intelligence? Who developed them?

5. Discuss language further. The article "Racist Use of the English Language" (see page 191) is an important resource for this.
   a. What is the difference between the expressions "culturally deprived" and "culturally exploited"?
   b. What is the difference between saying, "Masters used their slaves," and, "White captors raped the African women whom they held captive?"
   c. Why do we say that fighting for rights in 1776 was a "revolution" but that fighting for rights in 1968 by Black Americans was a "riot"?
   d. How is the English language used to cover up the real issues of racism?
6. Discuss how the English language affects one's self-image.
   a. What effect does language have on White children's self-image if they feel that white represents all that is "good" and black all that is "bad"?
   b. What is the effect on Black children's self-image?

Note to facilitator
1. People may try to "flight" by saying that words don't really matter or have any significance. It is vital to discuss how words communicate attitudes. There is a difference between calling someone who is Black a "nigger," and calling him or her a "Black person"—and between calling a Native American "an Injun" and calling the person a "Native American."
2. A second point to emphasize is how jokes—another form of language—perpetuate racism. By laughing at or telling a racist joke, we are supporting our own racism as well as others'. This point is vital and may also be met with resistance. The facilitator should try to make the point as clear as possible.

Time   25 minutes

Exercise 29   Cultural Differences: Black Is..., White Is....

Goals

1. To help participants become aware of cultural differences between Blacks and Whites.
2. To help participants see how different the Black experience is from the White experience.
3. To help participants understand some assumptions about cultural racism.

Materials needed

Books *Black Is . . .* and *White Is . . .* (page 198)

Instructions

1. Read each book aloud.
2. Discuss participants' reactions to the books.
3. Discuss examples of cultural racism.
   a. The "flesh-colored" bandage of *White Is . . ..*
   b. By whose standards are Third World people judged?
   c. What assumptions are made about Third World people by White society that could be seen as cultural racism, as presented in *Black Is . . .?*
   d. How does the American experience differ for Whites and for minorities?

Note to facilitator

1. If time does not permit you to read the books, be sure to have copies available so that participants can read them during breaks.
2. Use the books to focus on the inconsistencies in White American culture. The books clearly demonstrate the cultural differences between Black and White Americans, as well as the inconsistencies in American ideology.
3. Again raise the question, How are White standards used to judge others? Each book contains good examples showing how White people's assumptions are unfair as a basis on which to judge Third World people. Another question that should be raised is, How does the White culture negate the existence of Third World people?

4. It may be helpful to refer to some of the resources used in Stage 2—the selections by Buffy Saint Marie, Dick Gregory, and the Last Poets—who also share their views and perspectives on the effects of cultural racism on their peoples. This may further clarify the issues connected with cultural racism.

Time   20 minutes

Exercise 30　　Language: Cultural Racism at Its Extreme? The Klan

1. To clarify the ways in which language expresses and represents our attitudes.
2. To reveal the Klan as one means of perpetuating cultural racism.
3. To demonstrate the power of cultural racism as an underlying and ingrained part of our attitudes.

Tape *Join the Klan* (promotional tape, 1964) or
Film *Ku Klux Klan* (page 197)
Cassette player or 16-mm movie projector and screen

1. Play the tape *Join the Klan* or show the film *Ku Klux Klan.*
2. Have participants take special note of the language used, as well as the attitudes expressed. How are some of these same attitudes expressed (perhaps in different ways) by friends, relatives, government officials, and others? What is the difference between the two—the Klan members and those persons in our environment? How is patriotism presented on the tape? Religion? White people's rights? How are these ideologies discussed by others in America?
3. Have the participants discuss the Klan today.
   a. How does cultural racism support the Klan? Note that the ideology of the Klan underlies many of the norms and standards of today.
   b. How does institutional racism support the Klan?
   c. Why is the Klan still in existence today? What does that indicate about the White system?

Many people may not want to believe that the attitudes expressed on the tape or in the film still exist today. Have them review the integration of South Boston (1974–77) and the Klan's involvement there. It is important for them to realize that many of the same attitudes exist today, not only among Klan or John Birch Society members but also among "average" White Americans as well—college-dormitory residents, friends, relatives—perhaps some of the people in the workshop itself. You may want to consider attitudes on "reverse discrimination" with the Bakke case. It is important for participants to see that, unfortunately, such attitudes are not restricted to extremist groups.

Time   22 minutes (tape), 15 minutes (discussion)
1 hour (film), 30 minutes (discussion)

Exercise 31 Mini-Lecture: The Historical Roots of Cultural Racism

To help participants understand some of the historical roots of Whites and Blacks from which cultural racism developed.

Chart below on newsprint

1. Copy the chart below on newsprint.

Cultural Components of Africa and England, 1550–1600[1]

Cultural Component	Africa	England
Religion	Relativistic	Absolutist
	Pragmatic	Based on faith
	Magical	Moralistic
	Secular	Sacred
	Family-oriented	Privileged
Social organization	Matrilineal	Patriarchal
	Polygamous	Monogamous
	Status based on type of work	Status based on lack of need to work
	"Man is what he does"	"Man is what he owns"
	Stratified-fluid	Stratified-rigid
	Family discipline	Institutional discipline
Economics, property	Agrarian, artisan, commerce	Capitalist commerce
	Hunting, fishing	Artisan
	Collective property	Private property
Education	Informal (family, peers)	Formal (tutor, schools)
	Oral tradition	Written tradition

[1]Chart from J. Jones, *Prejudice and Racism*, p. 150.

Cultural Component	Africa	England
	Required interpersonal contact	Facilitated interpersonal separation
Time	Present, past fused	Past, future, no present
	Traditional (primitive)	Progress—positively evaluated change over time
	Little change over time	
Music	Rhythmic—body	Tonal, melodic—mind
	Songs secular	Songs sacred
World view	Intuitive, superstitious	Rational
	Tolerant, open	Intolerant, manipulative

2. Add to the chart or read the following excerpt (Jones, 1972, p. 149):

Englishmen of the sixteenth century were very ethnocentric and hence were predisposed to dislike or judge negatively any group of people who were different from themselves. Ethnocentrism is not, of course, a peculiarly British phenomenon, as most culture groups tend to think that their way is best. But within the context of English-African contact, British ethnocentrism was particularly salient: the culture of Africans was not merely different, but at the opposite end of the continuum on practically every major cultural criterion. Most significantly, British ethnocentrism included the glorification of the color white and the vilification of the color black. With the omniscience of historical perspective we might ask if there were any other way the contact of white Englishmen with black Africans could have turned out.

3. Discuss the following points:
   a. What are the implications of the English people's belief that the African culture was inferior to English culture in that it deviated from English norms?
   b. How is this ideology reflected in today's standards?

c. Which of the cultural differences shown in the chart have carried over into the dominant White American culture?
d. What implications do these standards have for those whose culture differs?
e. How are these standards reflected in:
(1) What is seen as beauty?
(2) What is seen as intelligence—mechanisms to measure it?
(3) What traditions are celebrated?
(4) What religion is most often practiced?
(5) What norms and values are generally accepted?

It is important for you to read *Prejudice and Racism* (Jones, 1972, pp. 149–68). This book is extremely helpful in developing the discussion of cultural differences. **Note to facilitator**

30 minutes **Time**

Exercise 32   IQ: The Dove Counter Balance Test

Goals   1. To have participants experience a culturally biased test to discover the racism inherent in standardized testing.
2. To explore IQ as a form of cultural racism.

Materials needed   Copies of the Dove Counter Balance Test (page 126)
Pens or pencils

Instructions   1. Hand out copies of the Dove Counter Balance Test.
2. Ask the participants to answer the thirty multiple-choice questions.
3. After the participants have completed the test, hand out the answer key so that they can correct their tests.
4. Discuss with the participants their reactions to taking the test.
5. Discuss IQ and how it both nourishes and is nourished by cultural racism.
6. How do culturally biased standards affect:
a. Admissions to colleges?
b. Employment?
c. Opportunities in education, including scholarships?

Note to facilitator   1. This exercise is designed to show that there is a cultural bias in "objective" tests. This is not a "Black intelligence test"; rather, it was developed to show that standardized tests favor one group over another.
2. It is important to focus on participants' feelings in taking the test. How did they feel when they answered a question wrong? When they answered one right? How did they feel in terms of relating to the material?
3. Discuss who develops standardized tests. What norms do the test-makers accept as givens? How are the norms of these tests de-

124

veloped? Which group do standardized tests help? Which groups do they hinder?
4. You may want to use a real standardized test to demonstrate how cultural racism operates. Often participants do not believe that these "objective tests" are culturally racist. Some specific examples are usually very convincing.
5. If the tape for Exercise 33 is unavailable, this exercise could be expanded to include some of the issues dealt with in that exercise.

45 minutes   **Time**

The Dove Counter Balance Test[1]

1. "T-Bone Walker" got famous for playing what?
   a) trombone
   b) piano
   c) "T-flute"
   d) guitar
   e) hambone
2. Whom did "Stagger Lee" kill (in the famous blues legend)?
   a) his mother
   b) Frankie
   c) Johnny
   d) his girl friend
   e) Billy
3. A "gas head" or "dupe" is a person who has
   a) a fast-moving car
   b) a stable of "lace"
   c) "process hair"
   d) a habit of stealing cars
   e) a long jail record for arson
4. If a man is called a "blood," then he is a
   a) fighter
   b) Mexican-American
   c) Black
   d) hungry hemophile
   e) Indian
5. If you throw the dice and "7" is showing on top, what is facing down?
   a) seven
   b) snake eyes
   c) boxcars
   d) little Joes
   e) eleven

---

[1] Developed by Adrian Dove in Watts, California.

6. Jazz pianist Ahmad Jamal took an Arabic name after becoming really famous. Previously, he had some fame with what he called his slave name. What was his previous name?
   a) Willie Lee Jackson
   b) LeRoi Jones
   c) Wilbur McDougal
   d) Fritz Jones
   e) Andy Johnson

7. In "C. C. Rider" what does the *C. C.* stand for?
   a) Civil Service
   b) Church Council
   c) Country Circuit preacher or an old-time rambler
   d) Country Club
   e) Cheatin' Charlie (the "Boxer Gunsel")

8. Cheap chitlings (not the kind you purchase frozen at a frozen-food counter) will taste rubbery unless they are cooked long enough. How soon can you quit cooking them to eat and enjoy them?
   a) 15 minutes
   b) 8 hours
   c) 24 hours
   d) 1 week (on a low flame)
   e) 1 hour

9. "Down Home" (the South) today, for the average "Soul Brother" who is picking cotton (in season from sunup to sundown), what is the average earning (take home) for one full day?
   a) $ .75
   b) $ .65
   c) $ 3.50
   d) $ 5.00
   e) $12.00

10. If a judge finds you guilty of "holding weed" (in California), what is the most he can give you?
   a) indeterminate (life)
   b) a nickel
   c) a dime
   d) a year in County
   e) $100.00

11. "Bird" or "Yardbird" was the "jacket that jazz lovers from coast to coast hung on," otherwise known as
    a) Lester Young
    b) Peggy Lee
    c) Benny Goodman
    d) Charlie Parker
    e) "Birdman of Alcatraz"

12. A "hype" is a person who
    a) always says he feels sickly
    b) has water on the brain
    c) uses heroin
    d) is always ripping and running
    e) is always sick

13. Hattie Mae Johnson is on the County. She has four children, and her husband is now in jail for nonsupport. Her welfare check is now $286.00 per month. Last night she went out with the biggest player in town. If she got pregnant, then nine months from now how much more will her welfare check be?
    a) $ 30.00
    b) $ 2.00
    c) $ 35.00
    d) $150.00
    e) $100.00

14. Hully Gully came from
    a) East Oakland
    b) Fillmore
    c) Watts
    d) Harlem
    e) Motor City

15. What is Willie Mae's last name?
    a) Schwartz
    b) Matauda
    c) Gomez
    d) Turner
    e) O'Flaherty

16. The opposite of square is
    a) round
    b) up
    c) down
    d) hip
    e) lame

17. Do the "Beatles" have soul?
    a) yes
    b) no
    c) gee whiz or maybe

18. A "handkerchief head" is
    a) a cool cat
    b) a porter
    c) an Uncle Tom
    d) a hoddi
    e) a preacher

19. What are the "Dixie Hummingbirds?"
    a) a part of the KKK
    b) a swamp disease
    c) a modern gospel group
    d) a Mississippi Black, paramilitary strike force
    e) deacons

20. "Jet" is
    a) an East Oakland motorcycle club
    b) one of the gangs in *West Side Story*
    c) a news and gossip magazine
    d) a way of life for the very rich

21. "Tell it . . .."
    a) like it think I am
    b) baby
    c) y'all
    d) like it is

22. "You've got to get up early in the morning if you want to . . .."
    a) catch the worms
    b) be healthy, wealthy, and wise
    c) try to fool me
    d) fare well
    e) be the first one on the street

23. And Jesus said, "Walk together, children, ..."
    a) don't you get weary. There's a great camp meeting
    b) for we shall overcome
    c) for the family that walks together talks together
    d) by your patience you will win your souls (Luke 21:9)
    e) find the things that are above, not the things that are on Earth (Col. 3:3)

24. "Money don't get everything, it's true . . .."
    a) but I don't have none and I'm so blue
    b) but what it don't get I can't use
    c) so make with what you've got
    d) but, I don't know that and neither do you

25. "Bo Diddley" is a
    a) camp for children
    b) cheap wine
    c) singer
    d) new dance
    e) mojo call

26. Which word is out of place here?
    a) splib
    b) muslim
    c) gray
    d) spook
    e) black

27. How much does a "short dog" cost?
    a) $ .15
    b) $2.00
    c) $ .55
    d) $ .05
    e) $ .86 plus tax

28. A "pimp" is also a young man who does not have a job.
    a) yes
    b) no
29. If a pimp is uptight with a woman who gets state aid, what does he mean when he talks about "Mother's Day?"
    a) second Sunday in May
    b) third Sunday in June
    c) first of every month
    d) none of these
    e) first and fifteenth of every month
30. Which one does not fit?
    a) *Guess Who's Coming to Dinner?*
    b) *Patch of Blue*
    c) *All the Young Men*
    d) *West Side Story*
    e) *The Defiant Ones*

Answer Key to Dove Counter Balance Test

1. D	11. D	21. D
2. E	12. C	22. C
3. C	13. C	23. A
4. C	14. E	24. B
5. A	15. D	25. C
6. D	16. D	26. C
7. C	17. B	27. C
8. C	18. C	28. A
9. D	19. C	29. C
10. C	20. C	30. D

Exercise 33   IQ: The Shockley-Poussaint Debate

Goals

1. To explore further the IQ issue.
2. To hear perspectives on the issue offered by William Bradford Shockley, a White professor at Stanford University, who advocates the theory that "Blacks are genetically inferior," and Alvin Poussaint, a Black professor at Harvard University, who opposes that theory.

Tape of debate between Shockley and Poussaint (page 198)   **Materials**
Cassette player   **needed**

1. Play the tape.   **Instructions**
2. Discuss the arguments presented by Shockley and Poussaint.
3. What are the implications of the system's support of people like Shockley? How does Shockley support and perpetuate White racism?
4. Repeat some of the questions listed in Exercise 32 relating to IQ.

1. This tape helps clarify issues involving IQ testing and the belief   **Note to**
   of some that Black people are genetically inferior to Whites. Partic-   **facilitator**
   ipants are often unsure what they really believe about this issue
   because the data seem confusing. They may read statistics that
   show that Blacks' IQ is 15 points lower than Whites'. If they do
   not understand why that is so—if they do not understand the
   formulation and nature of IQ tests—they will be unclear about
   what they believe. This exercise will help clarify this issue for
   them.
2. If the tape is unavailable, an extended discussion should take place
   in Exercise 32 of some of the issues mentioned in this exercise.
   The facilitator, being familiar with both groups' perspectives, can
   also spend some time discussing the implications of these theories.

1 hour (tape), 15–20 minutes (discussion)   **Time**

Stage 5   The Meaning of Whiteness: Individual Racism

Exercise 34   Adjective List: How I See Myself—My
                    Whiteness   page 139
                    Personal Checklist   141

          35   Being White in America Today Is Like   142

          36   White Is Beautiful   144

          37   Exploring Attitudes: Self-Image   146
                    "After You, My Dear Alphonse"   148

          38   Clarifying Attitudes   152
                    Values Clarification Exercise   154

          39   Exploration of Racist Attitudes   155
                    "Thirty Statements"   157
                    "Clarification of Thirty Statements"   159

          40   Assessing One's Understanding of
                    Racism   161
                    "A Vision of Equality"   163

          41   Discovering Inconsistencies Between
                    Attitudes and Behavior   164

See Appendix, pages 193 and 197, for readings and resources for Stage 5.

Stage 5   Individual Racism: The Meaning of Whiteness

Stage 5 brings us to one of the most crucial points in this training program. Earlier stages helped participants understand the dynamics of racism as it operates in White institutions and culture. At this stage they take another vital step in their exploration of racism as they translate those dynamics into their personal attitudes and behavior. They do so through exercises in which they:

1. Explore their White culture and develop a sense of positive identification of their whiteness.
2. Examine what it means to be White in a White racist society.
3. Focus on the inconsistencies in their own attitudes and behavior.
4. Explore how they may be perpetuating racism.

Participants enter Stage 5 having explored cultural racism and cultural differences. Although by this point they may understand that minority people may have different cultural perspectives from their own, they may not yet see themselves as Whites or identify their culture as the White culture. This issue *must* be examined and explored with participants.

Stage 5 helps participants discover and own their whiteness. Included in this exploration are such issues as: What is a White culture? Why do White people see themselves as individuals rather than as part of the White culture? What are the luxuries of being White in America? How do people feel about their whiteness? The main objective in exploring the issue of whiteness is for participants to realize that being White is important in one's life. Whatever ethnic group they may belong to, one of the determining factors of their fate in America is their whiteness. Being White makes them responsible for a system that is White and racist. Participants must also begin to understand in Stage 5 that because they are White and part of the racist system they have certain luxuries. Stage 5 names those luxuries and helps participants own their whiteness. Once they have taken this step, participants are on their way to exploring their own racism.

A second phase of Stage 5 focuses specifically on the individual's racism. By exploring attitudes and behaviors for inconsistencies, participants can begin to get in touch with their own racism. Just as it was important for participants to see the inconsistencies between American ideology and behaviors in institutions and culture, they must also recognize their own inconsistencies. The exercises facilitate this process by having them explore their own attitudes. They examine their attitudes toward Third World people, as well as ways in which conscious or unconscious attitudes may be perpetuating racism. The ways these attitudes develop are also examined.

To examine one's own behavior is a little more difficult. Part of the data will come from the participants' interactions in the group. There they can look at how their behavior has been either consistent or inconsistent with their attitudes. Participants also look at whether their behavior is perpetuating racism: Are they doing anything that is actively racist? How may their inaction be perpetuating and supporting racism? Participants reach the point where they can begin to name some inconsistencies between their attitudes and behavior and recognize how their behavior may be perpetuating racism. It is at this point that they begin to realize a need for change and develop a commitment to change. This prepares them for Stage 6, in which they will develop action strategies to combat racism.

Method   The role of the facilitator in Stage 5 does not differ greatly from that of the previous stages. This stage is very important in the training program. The facilitator must confront participants wherever possible with their racism, both attitudinal and behavioral. You can draw as well upon past stages to clarify and highlight participants' individual racism.

The first part of this stage centers on whiteness. One difficulty you may encounter is that participants may be somewhat at a loss about how to focus on their whiteness. They may understand that White people have a different culture from that of Blacks or Asian-Americans, but they may not be in touch with what the White culture is. In other words, they may know what they are not but not what they are. The facilitator has the task of helping them identify their White culture. One trap to be wary of is the reversion of some participants to their ethnic identities. Many people deny their whiteness by saying that their culture is derived from their ethnic identity. Although clearly that is a part of one's cultural identity and heritage, in America the overriding determiner of culture is one's color. Many White immigrants have suffered discrimination, it is true, but because of their color they and their families have ultimately been accepted. Racial minorities, such as Blacks, Native Americans, Chicanos, and Asian-Americans, on the other hand, have been discriminated against in the United States for hundreds of years and are still at the bottom of the socioeconomic ladder. The ability to "make it" in the system is dependent on one's color, not one's ethnic background or abilities. People can hide their ethnic identity but not usually their racial identity. This reality must be examined in the group.

A second dynamic in the group may be the denial of responsibility for racism: "I'm not responsible for what my ancestors did." This attitude should be explored in terms of the luxuries Whites have because of the racist nature of the system and the reality that Whites maintain, support, and perpetuate the system.

Another part of this stage explores individual racism through one's attitudes and behaviors and tries to uncover inconsistencies in them. The facilitator's role here is to help participants honestly discuss their real attitudes as well as understand the reasons why an attitude and/or behavior may be racist.

Finally, this stage may bring guilt feelings to the surface again, perhaps deeper ones than those expressed in Stage 3. The role of the facilitator is crucial at this point. The facilitator must help participants work through these feelings because they are a form of self-indulgence indicating that they are feeling sorry for themselves. Guilt serves as a stopping force, preventing people from moving forward and taking action. Participants must understand that their guilt benefits no one. It is important that they feel some internal conflict and responsibility, and these valid feelings should be supported. But the guilt needs to be transformed into a motivating force that will enable them to take constructive steps to combat racism instead of just feeling guilty about their role in it. This energy for action is vital for Stage 6.

Exercise 34 Adjective List: How I See Myself— My Whiteness

Goals

1. To help participants begin to explore how they see themselves as Whites.
2. To explore seeing oneself as an individual as opposed to seeing oneself as part of a group.

Materials needed

Copies of Personal Checklist (page 141)
Pens or pencils
Newsprint
Felt markers
Masking tape

Instructions

1. Hand out copies of the Personal Checklist to the participants.
2. Ask them to select from the list five words that they feel best describe themselves. If they feel that the appropriate words are not on the list, have them add words with which they feel comfortable.
3. Ask several participants to share their words. Write the words on newsprint. Note how many people in the group had the same words on their lists.
4. Ask the participants to return to the Personal Checklist. Ask them now to select from the list five words that describe them racially. Again, if they feel that the appropriate words are not there, have them add others.
5. Ask them to share their lists, noting whether they changed any words on their second lists. Write the changed words on the newsprint. Note how many people in the group changed their lists and the kinds of changes.
6. Discuss the following:
   a. How did the participants feel while developing each list?
   b. Why did they change their lists?
   c. Why do people see themselves differently when referring to themselves as part of the White race?

139

d. What does that say about White people, in that Whites see themselves as individuals first?

Note to facilitator 1. You may want to discuss the individual-group issue—that is, that White people do not have to see themselves as White. They have the luxury of seeing themselves as individuals, whereas people who are oppressed by the system can never forget who they are racially. A Black person wakes up every day aware first that he or she is Black and only second as an individual within that group. (It may be interesting to see whether women participants list words indicating awareness of belonging to an oppressed group in the United States as compared to the men's word lists. This dynamic can highlight the racial issue.) The important thing to stress here is that a member of an oppressed group needs the support of that group, whereas the oppressor does not need the group's support. Third World people see themselves as part of a group first, whereas White people see themselves as individuals first.
2. Many people often do not like such checklists because they feel pigeonholed and categorized. It is helpful to acknowledge that it is hard to define oneself in only five words and to emphasize that they are to pick words that best seem to identify themselves.
3. It is useful not to tell participants the goal of this exercise before beginning it. Participants' lists change when they realize that they will have to define themselves racially after they define themselves the first time. Therefore, to gain the full impact of this exercise, give each direction separately, as suggested.
4. You may want to add your own words or develop a list of words that you feel are appropriate to your own groups.

Time   30 minutes

Personal Checklist

1. Select five (5) words from the list below that best describe you:

accepted	dying	liberal	schizophrenic
adaptive	easy	limited	scientific
afraid	emotional	misunderstood	secure
Afro	employed	nice	select
arrogant	enraged	normal	selective
assaulted	exploited	oppressed	separatist
average	flexible	oppressive	sexual
bad	free	outraged	sharp
beautiful	friendly	paternal	sister
better	good	patient	soft
big	happy	people	soulful
blamed	helpless	poor	strong
brave	hopeful	powerful	supportive
brother	humble	privileged	tight
brutal	hungry	proper	together
chosen	hurt	protective	tokenized
Christian	independent	protestant	tracked
confident	individual	proud	true
conservative	inferior	pure	undereducated
controller	insulted	puzzled	underemployed
creative	intelligent	religious	understanding
denied	invisible	respected	unemotional
determined	just	rich	up-tight
dignified	knowledgeable	right	victimized
disappointed	leader	ripped-off	worthy

2. Write any additional words if the above word list is not descriptive
   enough to reflect your true feelings:

Exercise 35　　Being White in America Today
　　　　　　　　Is Like . . ..[1]

Goals　　1. To point out luxuries White people have by virtue of their white-
　　　　　　ness.
　　　　　2. To illustrate differences between the White and the Black ex-
　　　　　　periences in America today.

Materials　Newsprint
needed　　Felt markers
　　　　　Masking tape

Instructions　1. Write the statement "Being White in America today is like . . .."
　　　　　　　on newsprint.
　　　　　　2. Ask the participants to complete the statement three or four times
　　　　　　　in a few words. Go around the group, asking the participants to
　　　　　　　share one of their responses. Write the responses on newsprint.
　　　　　　3. After the participants have shared their lists, have them clarify
　　　　　　　and discuss their sentences.
　　　　　　4. Go around the circle again. Using the same responses, ask the
　　　　　　　participants to explain the sentence with only one change: sub-
　　　　　　　stituting *Black* for *White* so that the sentence now reads, "Being
　　　　　　　Black in America today is like . . .." Discuss the different mean-
　　　　　　　ings the sentence takes on with that one word change.
　　　　　　5. Discuss the following:
　　　　　　　a. In America how does being White differ from being Black?
　　　　　　　b. What luxuries do we as White people seem to have?

Note to　　1. You can change the participants' second sentence, substituting any
facilitator　　other minority group with whom they are somewhat familiar—
　　　　　　　Native American, Chicano, or Asian-American.

[1] Adapted from an exercise developed by Pat A. Bidol and R. C. Weber, *Developing
New Perspectives on Race: An Innovative Multimedia Social Studies Curriculum in
Race Relations for Secondary Level.*

2. It is important to acknowledge that we as Whites can never really know what it is like to be a minority person in this country but that we do know some of the differences between White people's and minority people's experiences. The facilitator must stress that we as Whites will never be able to experience what minority people experience in America today.
3. If participants do not discern some of the luxuries that White people have, strongly encourage the group to explore this issue. It is essential for participants to be in touch with the benefits they receive from the system.

45 minutes   **Time**

Exercise 36   White Is Beautiful[1]

Goals   1. To explore what it means to be White in America.
2. To explore participants' feelings about being White.
3. To facilitate participants' acceptance of their whiteness.

Materials needed   Paper
Pens or pencils

Instructions   1. Ask the participants to take ten minutes to respond to the slogan, "White Is Beautiful." Ask them to think about what it means to them personally.
2. Ask the participants to share their responses.
3. Discuss the following:
  a. How did the participants feel responding to, "White Is Beautiful"?
  b. What difficulties did they encounter?
  c. What do their difficulties say about how we as White people see ourselves?
  d. What is the White culture?
  e. How do people feel about being part of that White culture?
  f. Do they resist identifying with the White culture? Why?

Note to facilitator   1. This exercise often brings to the surface a large number of guilt feelings about being White and about having luxuries Whites have and/or being aware of one's inaction and therefore the perpetuation of racism. Explore this guilt, helping participants see that it is not helpful or healthy. It is important that they identify the source of the guilt—feeling sorry for oneself for being White. Participants will begin to realize that their guilt does not accom-

---

[1] Adapted from an exercise developed by Frederick R. Preston, University of Massachusetts.

144

plish anything constructive but is only a burden on them. That will help them realize the importance of taking active steps to rid themselves of the burden.

2. Participants may find it difficult to identify the elements of White culture. Explore why it is difficult and help them delineate the elements of White culture as a group if they cannot do it individually.

3. This exercise can lead to further examination of the privileges of being White, as well as ways in which Whites unconsciously perpetuate racism.

4. You should also help the group identify positive aspects of being White. It is important for them to feel good about themselves as White people. All too often Whites deny their whiteness because they feel that being White is negative.

30 minutes   **Time**

Exercise 37   Exploring Attitudes: Self-Image[1]

Goals
1. To explore how prejudiced attitudes work to support one's self-image.
2. To explore further how individual racism operates in White attitudes.

Materials needed
Story "After You, My Dear Alphonse," by Shirley Jackson (page 148)
Paper
Pens or pencils

Instructions
1. Read the story "After You, My Dear Alphonse" to the group.
2. Ask the participants to discuss the assumptions and prejudices displayed in Mrs. Wilson's attitudes and actions. What do her attitudes and assumptions do for her self-image?
3. Ask the participants to write down one of their negative attitudes, or prejudices, that is racist, for example, "I would never marry a Black person," or, "Blacks are not as smart as Whites."
4. Ask the participants to develop an advertisement designed to "sell" that prejudice to others. Include what owning that prejudice can do for you, what it can do for others, and so on.
5. Have participants share their prejudices and advertisements.
6. Discuss the following:
   a. What do our attitudes support in us?
   b. How do our attitudes help foster certain perspectives of ourselves?

Note to facilitator
1. This exercise begins the second phase of Stage 5. Participants will begin to look at their own attitudes and behaviors and examine them for inconsistencies.

---

[1]Exercise developed by Carole Betsch.

2. This exercise also helps participants begin thinking about the relationships their attitudes have to their self-image. If the participants can get in touch with the purpose for which they hold an attitude, they can better understand it and perhaps change it.
3. Exercise 37 facilitates participants' exploration of assumptions. What assumptions do Whites make about Third World people? How do we act on those assumptions? How do those assumptions often center on or support racism?
4. Finally, this exercise helps participants understand paternalistic racism. Why does Mrs. Wilson *need* to *help* Boyd? Discuss paternalistic racism as a form of racism in which White liberals treat minority people as children who have no responsibility or sense. Paternalistic racism causes Whites to feel that they must be the ones to help even when their help is not asked for.

25 minutes   **Time**

After You, My Dear Alphonse[1]

Mrs. Wilson was just taking the gingerbread out of the oven when she heard Johnny outside talking to someone. "Johnny," she called, "you're late. Come in and get your lunch."

"Just a minute, Mother," Johnny said. "After you, my dear Alphonse."

"After *you,* my dear Alphonse," another voice said.

"No, after *you,* my dear Alphonse," Johnny said.

Mrs. Wilson opened the door. "Johnny," she said, "you come in this minute and get your lunch. You can play after you've eaten."

Johnny came in after her, slowly. "Mother," he said, "I brought Boyd home for lunch with me."

"Boyd?" Mrs. Wilson thought for a moment. "I don't believe I've met Boyd. Bring him in, dear, since you've invited him. Lunch is ready."

"Boyd!" Johnny yelled. "Hey, Boyd, come on in!"

"I'm coming. Just got to unload this stuff."

"Well, hurry, or my mother'll be sore."

"Johnny, that's not very polite to either your friend or your mother," Mrs. Wilson said. "Come sit down, Boyd."

As she turned to show Boyd where to sit, she saw he was a Negro boy, smaller than Johnny but about the same age. His arms were loaded with split kindling wood. "Where'll I put this stuff, Johnny?" he asked.

Mrs. Wilson turned to Johnny. "Johnny," she said, "What did you make Boyd do? What is that wood?"

"Dead Japanese," Johnny said mildly, "We stand them in the ground and run over them with tanks."

"How do you do, Mrs. Wilson?" Boyd said.

"How do you do, Boyd? You shouldn't let Johnny make you carry all that wood. Sit down now and eat lunch, both of you."

[1]From Shirley Jackson, *The Lottery*, New York: Popular Library, 1975.

148

"Why shouldn't he carry the wood, Mother? It's his wood. We got it at his place."

"Johnny," Mrs. Wilson said, "go on and eat your lunch."

"Sure," Johnny said. He held out the dish of scrambled eggs to Boyd. "After you, my dear Alphonse," Johnny said.

"After *you,* my dear Alphonse," Boyd said.

"After *you,* my dear Alphonse," Johnny said. They began to giggle.

"Are you hungry, Boyd?" Mrs. Wilson asked.

"Yes, Mrs. Wilson."

"Well, don't let Johnny stop you. He always fusses about eating so you just see that you get a good lunch. There's plenty of food here for you to have all you want."

"Thank you, Mrs. Wilson."

"Come on, Boyd," Johnny said. He pushed half the scrambled eggs onto Boyd's plate. Boyd watched while Mrs. Wilson put a dish of stewed tomatoes beside his plate.

"Boyd don't eat tomatoes, do you, Boyd?" Johnny said.

"Doesn't eat tomatoes, Johnny. And just because you don't like them, don't say that about Boyd. Boyd will eat *anything.* "

"Bet he won't," Johnny said, attacking his scrambled eggs.

"Boyd wants to grow up and be a big strong man so he can work hard," Mrs. Wilson said. "I'll bet Boyd's father eats stewed tomatoes."

"My father eats anything he wants to," Boyd said.

"So does mine," Johnny said. "Sometimes he doesn't eat hardly anything. He's a little guy, though. Wouldn't hurt a flea."

"Mine's a little guy, too," Boyd said.

"I'll bet he's strong, though," Mrs. Wilson said. She hesitated. "Does he . . . work?"

"Sure," Johnny said. "Boyd's father works in a factory."

"There, you see?" Mrs. Wilson said. "And he certainly has to be strong to do that—all that lifting and carrying at a factory."

"Boyd's father doesn't have to," Johnny said. "He's a foreman."

Mrs. Wilson felt defeated. "What does your mother do, Boyd?"

"My mother?" Boyd was surprised. "She takes care of us kids."

"Oh. She doesn't work, then?"

"Why should she?" Johnny said through a mouthful of eggs. "You don't work."

"You really don't want any stewed tomatoes, Boyd?"

"No, thank you, Mrs. Wilson," Boyd said.

"No, thank you, Mrs. Wilson, no, thank you, Mrs. Wilson, no, thank you, Mrs. Wilson," Johnny said. "Boyd's sister's going to work, though. She's going to be a teacher."

"That's a very fine attitude for her to have, Boyd," Mrs. Wilson restrained an impulse to pat Boyd on the head. "I imagine you're all very proud of her?"

"I guess so," Boyd said.

"What about all your other brothers and sisters? I guess all of you want to make just as much of yourselves as you can."

"There's only me and Jean," Boyd said. "I don't know yet what I want to be when I grow up."

"We're going to be tank drivers, Boyd and me," Johnny said.

"Zoom." Mrs. Wilson caught Boyd's glass of milk as Johnny's napkin ring suddenly transformed into a tank, plowed heavily across the table.

"Look, Johnny," Boyd said. "Here's a foxhole. I'm shooting at you."

Mrs. Wilson, with the speed born of long experience, took the gingerbread off the shelf and placed it carefully between the tank and the foxhole.

"Now eat as much as you want to, Boyd," she said. "I want to see you get filled up."

"Boyd eats a lot, but not as much as I do," Johnny said. "I'm bigger than he is."

"You're not much bigger," Boyd said. "I can beat you running."

Mrs. Wilson took a deep breath. "Boyd, Johnny has some suits that are a little too small for him, and a winter coat. It's not new, of course, but there's lots of wear in it still. And I have a few dresses that your mother or sister could probably use. Your mother can make them over into lots of things for all of you, and I'd be very happy to give them to you. Suppose before you leave I make up a big bundle and then you and Johnny can take it over to your mother right away. . . ." Her voice trailed off as she saw Boyd's puzzled expression.

"But I have plenty of clothes, thank you," he said. "And I don't think my mother knows how to sew very well, and anyway

150

I guess we buy about everything we need. Thank you very much, though."

"We don't have time to carry that old stuff around, Mother," Johnny said. "We got to play tanks with the kids today."

Mrs. Wilson lifted the plate of gingerbread off the table as Boyd was about to take another piece. "There are many little boys like you, Boyd, who would be very grateful for the clothes someone was kind enough to give them."

"Boyd will take them if you want him to, Mother," Johnny said.

"I didn't mean to make you mad, Mrs. Wilson," Boyd said.

"Don't think I'm angry, Boyd. I'm just disappointed in you, that's all. Now let's not say anything more about it."

She began clearing the plates off the table, and Johnny took Boyd's hand and pulled him to the door. "Bye, Mother," Johnny said. Boyd stood for a minute, staring at Mrs. Wilson's back.

"After you, my dear Alphonse," Johnny said, holding the door open.

"Is your mother still mad?" Mrs. Wilson heard Boyd ask in a low voice.

"I don't know," Johnny said. "She's screwy sometimes."

"So's mine," Boyd said. He hesitated. "After *you,* my dear Alphonse."

Exercise 38   Clarifying Attitudes

Goals
1. To help participants get in touch with their values centering on racism.
2. To help participants identify their attitudes and behavior in a racial situation.
3. To highlight inaction as a perpetuation of racism.

Materials needed
Values Clarification Exercise (page 154)
Paper
Pens or pencils

Instructions
1. Read the Values Clarification Exercise to the group.
2. Ask the participants to rank from 1 to 6 according to their values who was "most wrong" to "most right" in the exercise.
3. Divide the group into small groups of four to six persons. Have individuals share their lists, and then have the group develop a list that all of them agree on.
4. Have the small groups share their lists with the large group. Have them also share their reasons for their choices.
5. Discuss the differences in the lists and the values represented.

Note to facilitator
1. This exercise can be changed to make it appropriate for the specific situation. It is essential, however, for the values of the six people in the exercise to be somewhat close to those represented in the Values Clarification Exercise. The characters and the values they represent in this exercise are:

Bill—goes through the system to achieve his goals.
Head of residence—holds the power, gives the OK, then, when he is under pressure, reneges; is responsible for the situation in that he could have averted it if he had used the power he had.

Art—states his racist opinion openly; it is easier for Black students to deal with him, because they know where he stands.

Ernie—inactive; although he is supportive of the Black students' issue, they don't know it; he could influence other White students, but he does not use his power. His silence supports the racism of other Whites.

John—violent, blatantly and destructively racist.

Suzanne—violent in retaliation—out of frustration and anger.

2. This exercise dramatizes the issues of power, violence, and inaction. It helps clarify and assess participants' real attitudes—whether they reflect an understanding of racism. The processing of this exercise can confront participants with inconsistencies in their expressed attitudes and their actual choices.

3. Share with the group the information about the characters given above after the report—out of each group. Does this information produce any change in the participants' original lists?

35 minutes   **Time**

Values Clarification Exercise[1]

The setting is a college dorm.

Bill, a Black student, lives in the dorm. No Black studies courses are offered in his subject area. He goes through the regular university procedures to obtain funds, approval, and a faculty member for a Black studies course. Fifteen Black students sign up. Bill goes to his head of residence and asks if they can use the TV room on Monday nights since that is the only time the professor is free. The TV room is the only room in the dorm with audiovisual equipment.

The head of residence approves the request.

Monday night arrives. The Black students go to the TV room and find a group of White students watching a football game. A heated discussion ensues.

Art, a White student, yells out, "You God damn niggers go back where you came from!"

Ernie, a White student, believes that the Black students are right, since the TV room is the only place they have to meet. He does not say anything, however.

The Black students leave. Bill later goes to the head of residence to explain what happened. The head of residence replies: "I made a mistake. The TV room really serves a need for all students. Since there are only fifteen students, find another place."

The next Monday night the Black students go to the TV room early and begin class.

The White students come in, and again a heated exchange takes place. John, a White student, runs upstairs to one of the Black students' rooms and, using a passkey, enters the room and throws books and clothes on the floor. Suzanne, a Black student in the class, hears about John and picks up a book and throws it through the TV.

[1]Developed by Joel Goodman, University of Massachusetts.

154

Exercise 39   Exploration of Racist Attitudes[1]

Goals

1. To help participants become aware of racist attitudes they presently accept or previously accepted.
2. To explore the myths behind some of these attitudes.
3. To help participants understand how and why these attitudes are racist.

Materials needed

Copies of "Thirty Statements" (page 157)
Pens or pencils

Instructions

1. Have the participants fill out the "Thirty Statements" sheet, putting an X before those statements that represent their present attitudes and an 0 before those statements that represent previously held attitudes. They are to leave blank those attitudes they have never held.
2. Have participants share their responses, indicating why they changed previously held attitudes or why they maintain present attitudes and how they feel about them. The role of the facilitator and the group is to clarify the racism in each of the statements (see page 159).
3. Discuss the participants' reactions.
   a. Do they understand why a given statement is racist?
   b. On what myths are the attitudes based?

Note to facilitator

1. This exercise is long and can become somewhat tedious if each statement is discussed. It may be useful to ask participants to choose those statements that are of particular importance to them now.
2. This exercise always seems to clarify much of the participants' confusion. They have heard and believed many of the attitudes expressed in the statements, and the explanations help them adjust

[1] Adapted from an exercise developed by James M. Edler.

155

their perspectives and develop a better understanding of the racism in the attitudes.

3. Obviously the facilitator must also be aware of the subtler issues of racism in the statements.

Time   1 hour

Thirty Statements[1]

_____ 1. What do they want?

_____ 2. I don't understand what you people are saying.

_____ 3. On the whole, the educated, the upper classes, the emotionally mature, and the deeply religious are much less racist.

_____ 4. Other ethnic groups had to struggle. Why is this so different?

_____ 5. Angry minorities make me feel so helpless.

_____ 6. Racism exists only where minorities exist.

_____ 7. (To a minority) "No matter what I say, it doesn't suit you."

_____ 8. If you could just get people feeling good about themselves, there would be much less racism.

_____ 9. Black Power means violence.

_____ 10. I'm not a racist, but when it comes right down to it, I wouldn't marry a Black person.

_____ 11. I should not be held responsible for the actions of my ancestors.

_____ 12. I'm with them up to the point where they (want to) break the law.

_____ 13. These days whenever a minority person sneezes, thirty-seven White people rush up to wipe his nose.

_____ 14. Minority members must be present in order for Whites to make progress.

_____ 15. How can I be pro-Black without being anti-White?

_____ 16. I do not personally have responsibility for the policies of racist institutions.

_____ 17. The most important things minorities need are education and the vote.

_____ 18. (White) people should not have to integrate if they don't want to.

[1]Developed by Gerald Weinstein, Leonard Smith, and James Edler, University of Massachusetts.

_____ 19. Love cannot be legislated.

_____ 20. What are we going to do to alleviate the Black problem?

_____ 21. Every person should be judged solely on his or her accomplishments, regardless of race.

_____ 22. Because of the civil-rights legislation of the past twenty years, Blacks have greater responsibility to exploit the opportunities made available to them.

_____ 23. We (Whites) should get a little more appreciation for what we are doing to help.

_____ 24. (Said to a Black person) I've gotten to know you so well that I just don't see you as Black any more.

_____ 25. Some of my best friends are Black.

_____ 26. They don't want us to deal with their problems.

_____ 27. Every time I express my opinion to a Black person, I get put down.

_____ 28. On the basis of statistics it's true that there is a higher crime rate in the ghetto.

_____ 29. Black people are more aware of their feelings.

_____ 30. In many situations minorities are paranoid and oversensitive, they read more into the situation than is really there.

Clarification of the Thirty Statements

Below are descriptions of the racist assumptions in some of the statements:

Statements	Assumptions
1 and 2	Feigns ignorance of legitimate minority demands for the basic ideals of all people—justice, equity, pluralism, human-heartedness, etc.
3	Assumes that racism is an individual matter rather than one of all Whites who partake of the benefits of a White racist society.
4	Shows a deep ignorance of the special deprivations suffered by Black people because of Whites.
5	A "copout" from White responsibility for dealing with White racism. The statement blames minorities for making Whites feel helpless—a special example of "blaming the victim."
8	Denies the fact of institutional racism and every White person's responsibility to combat it.
9	False; Black Power is necessary for pluralism, equity, etc. It means the ability to have pride in oneself and one's culture, as well as self-determination.
10	A contradiction—self-evident.
11	Avoids Whites' current responsibility to deal with current racism. We are all guilty by failing to take action and/or by partaking of the benefits of a White racist society.
13	Denies or minimizes how little things have changed for minorities in basic ways.
15	Assumes that there can be no true pluralism.
18 and 19	Deny legitimate human rights by treating the problem as one of individuals' feelings.
20	It's a *White* problem.
21	This is a statement for equality rather than for equity

and can perpetuate racism by systematically ignoring the larger amount of investment required by Blacks to attain the same accomplishments because of White racism.

23   Should a child beater be appreciated when he beats less hard? *Justice* is appreciated.
24   Denies blackness.
25   Insidious patronizing attitude; suggests a superior position of the White person.
26   Injustice, etc., are not "their" problems but Whites' problems.
28   Blaming the victim does not adequately account for what White institutions have done to produce those results.

Exercise 40 Assessing One's Understanding of Individual Racism

Goals

1. To assess participants' understanding of whiteness and racism.
2. To help participants see inconsistencies in attitudes that are racist.
3. To further participants' understanding and owning of whiteness.

Materials needed

Copies of "A Vision of Equality" (page 163)
Pens or pencils

Instructions

1. Ask participants to read "A Vision of Equality."
2. Ask them to underline the assumptions (implicit and/or explicit) with which they agree.
3. Ask them to share their underlined statements.
4. Discuss the following:
   a. What are the assumptions that are being made?
   b. Why do you agree with them?
5. Issues to be covered include:
   a. The writer's belief in the American myths
      My parents could make it
      America, land of opportunity
      I've had to work hard
      The melting-pot theory
   b. The writer's denial of his or her whiteness
      Wanting to be seen as different from other whites
      Not wanting to be stereotyped
      Anger at the system for being classified
   c. The writer's inconsistencies (not wanting people to divide themselves and then discussing "black and white")
   d. The writer's lack of awareness and understanding of institutional racism—"handouts"—reverse racism; wanting a society based on quality and individuality

Note to facilitator

1. This rebuttal is loaded with racist assumptions. Many participants still find themselves struggling with their whiteness. This exer-

cise helps them understand how their whiteness has served to their advantage in accruing benefits of the system. By denying one's whiteness and the importance of color in "getting ahead," one is also denying his or her racism.

2. It is also critical to note once again the reliance on and belief in the American myths. It is necessary to highlight the discrepancies between ideology and behavior.

Time   45 minutes

Underline the assumptions (implicit and explicit) with which you agree.

A Vision of Equality[1]

I'm a person too. I'm tired of being told I'm responsible for the sins of my ancestors. Why, my family didn't arrive in this country until after World War II. They were oppressed in Europe and came to America seeking opportunity and a better life.

My parents worked hard, and I've had to work hard too. No one gave me a handout to get through college. Since my family couldn't afford to send me, I supported myself. Now, after all my hard work, I turn around and a less well qualified minority is getting the job I deserve.

I agree that minorities have been discriminated against. But now we're discriminating in reverse. I feel that I'm being lumped together, stereotyped. My humanity is being denied. My individuality is just as important to me as it is to minorities. I'm all for equality, but let's make it both ways.

It disturbs me to see people dividing themselves. We've got to learn to get along with each other, and the only way we can do that is by treating each other as individuals, not as black or white. People are people, and once we realize that, we can achieve a society which rewards quality and individuality.

[1] Developed in collaboration with Glenn S. Phillips, University of Oklahoma.

Exercise 41   Discovering Inconsistencies Between Attitudes and Behavior

Goals   1. To identify one's values and attitudes centering on racism.
               2. To explore one's behavior based on those values.
               3. To discover inconsistencies between values and behavior.

Materials   Paper
needed   Pens or pencils

Instructions 1. Ask participants to take a piece of paper and divide it into four
                 columns, headed as follows:

I	II	III	IV
Values/Attitudes	Actions I Have Taken	Consistency	

2. Ask participants to think of one positive anti-racist attitude or
   value they hold in connection with racism, for example, "Whites
   are responsible for racism." List this attitude in column I.
3. Ask participants to list in column II specific actions they have
   taken on that attitude: "I have tried to reeducate my friend about
   his or her racism"; or, "I have pushed for more Third World
   representation in city government as a result of Third World
   people's expressed needs" (if none, they are to leave the column
   blank).
4. Tell the participants that if they have taken actions that seem
   consistent with that attitude, they are to check column III (if not,
   they are to leave the column blank).
5. Participants are to leave column IV blank for now (it will be
   completed in Stage 6, Exercise 42).
6. Discuss the lists. Ask the participants what they learned about
   their attitudes and behaviors? Participants can then complete the
   first three columns outside the workshop.

164

1. This exercise can also be expanded into a journal. Have partici- **Note to** pants list their positive attitudes about being anti-racist. Have them **facilitator** record for one week their behaviors that are consistent with that attitude and those that are inconsistent. This activity helps participants see for themselves the gaps between behavior and attitude and will help them recognize their individual racism.
2. It is important to emphasize that this exercise focuses on positive anti-racist attitudes. It may also be necessary to emphasize how often people act on their racist attitudes in a similar manner. This exercise can be adapted for that goal as well.
3. The exercise leads into Stage 6, in which participants will be developing action strategies to combat racism.

25 minutes   **Time**

Exercise 42   Developing Action on
              Personal Inconsistencies   page 169

        43   Commitment to Combat Racism   170
                Sheet 1   171
                Sheet 2   173

        44   The Costs and Benefits of Dealing with Racism 174
                "What Would I Give Up by Acting Against
                Racism?"   176

        45   Dealing with Racism: Role Plays   177

        46   Strategy and Action Planning   178
                "Strategy and Action Plan"   180

        47   Evaluation and Feedback   181
                Feedback Sheet: Course and Facilitator
                Evaluation   182

        48   Closing   183

See Appendix, pages 195 and 197, for readings and resources for Stage 6.

Stage 6   Developing Action Strategies

This training program and the theory behind it are directed toward this final stage. Unless this stage is achieved, little has been accomplished. Stage 6 concentrates on defining and developing action strategies to combat racism. The goal is to move participants to becoming "anti-racist racists." To help reach this goal, the exercises in this stage are designed to:

1. Help participants explore possible action strategies.
2. Help participants define and develop a specific course of action to combat racism.
3. Help participants develop an ongoing support base.
4. Help participants name the next steps for their continued exploration of personal racism.

In this last stage one clear objective must be met if the training program is to be successful. Participants must leave it willing and ready to take action against racism. This phase is called "becoming an anti-racist racist." An anti-racist racist is a White person who understands his or her racism, understands that, given the dynamics of racism in the United States today, he or she will always be racist, but takes action to try to combat it in situations where he or she has some power. In other words, an anti-racist racist is one who takes action to try to solve the White problem. The most important point of this training program is that *inaction is racism*. We Whites must not only understand our racism—how it developed and how it operates in our society and in our personal lives—but *do* something with that knowledge that will effect some change in our racist system. That is the essence of the last stage—and the purpose of the entire training program.

To help participants meet the challenge of taking action steps to combat racism, the facilitator must focus on the costs and benefits of taking such action. Participants must explore "what's in it for them," including the risks and the benefits. Once participants understand the price they pay either for action or for inaction, they can

167

explore possible action projects. They must be willing to make a commitment to specific action. Once that commitment is made, the initial steps must be defined so that participants have a clear direction about how to begin. A vital part of this process includes the development of a support base. Often the workshop group itself serves this function.

A second important goal of this final stage is to assure that, when the participants end the formal workshop experience, their personal exploration of racism will not end. Racism is so deeply ingrained in us that clearly one workshop cannot uncover all its aspects or teach us all that there is to know about it. Participants leave with the task of continuing to learn about racism on all levels. Stage 6 is designed to help participants name their next steps in that exploration. These steps may include reading more about the subject, taking a course on one particular aspect of the workshop, or joining an interracial group. The important thing participants must understand is that racism is not easily solved or even identified. A commitment of time and energy is necessary if one truly wants to become anti-racist.

Method In this last stage the facilitator has one basic task: to assure that each participant is clear on goals for the future. The facilitator can help participants develop their goals by breaking down some of the possible action projects into clear and specific steps. Participants need to understand that their actions need not be grand gestures and that they should start with a reachable goal. Clearly they can change neither themselves nor the system overnight. One way a facilitator can help in this process is to inform the participants about specific activities that are already underway in the community. This information may help the participants become involved and also provide an established support base. To encourage the participants to explore further their personal racism, the facilitator should share his or her knowledge of specific resources that can give participants a clear direction. These resources may include other workshops, materials, books, records, resource people, and courses.

The facilitator must make the group aware that the end of the workshop marks not the end of a process but rather the beginning. If the participants fail to take action on what they have learned, they have not moved at all. If they commit themselves to take action and meet that commitment, they are beginning the long, sometimes hard road to liberation. The challenge to the facilitator is to impress this point on all the participants.

168

Exercise 42   Developing Action on Personal Inconsistencies

1. To help participants develop action strategies that will close the gaps between the inconsistencies in their attitudes and behavior.   **Goals**
2. To help participants define their next steps in their exploration of personal racism.

Sheets developed in Exercise 41—"Discovering Inconsistencies Between Attitudes and Behavior"   **Materials needed**
Pens or pencils

1. Participants should have the sheets they began in Exercise 41.   **Instructions**
2. Ask them to title column IV "Actions I Can Take" and then list actions they can take to make their behavior more consistent with their attitudes or further actions they can take to give more support to their anti-racist attitudes.
3. Have them share their lists with the group.
4. Ask them to star one action on the list that they *want* to take.

This exercise helps participants define some actions they can take to counter their personal racism. They should be encouraged to consider not only direct but also indirect forms of action. Indirect action may include finding ways to learn more about one's racism and its dynamics, asking someone to serve as a process observer and give feedback about how consistent their behavior is with their attitudes, or keeping a journal of behavior and reviewing it weekly for consistency and a regular development of possible actions.   **Note to facilitator**

40 minutes   **Time**

Goals	1. To assess participants' commitment to combat racism.
	2. To help participants generate ideas about actions they can take.

Materials needed
Copies of "Commitment to Combat Racism," sheets 1 and 2 (pages 171 and 173)
Pens or pencils

Instructions
1. Hand out copies of "Commitment to Combat Racism," sheet 1.
2. Ask participants to check those items on which they have taken action.
3. Ask them to share their lists.
4. Discuss the following:
   a. Reactions to the list and the items.
   b. The kinds of actions that can be taken on institutional and personal levels.
5. Hand out copies of "Commitment to Combat Racism," sheet 2. Develop through brainstorming additional kinds of actions that can be taken.

Note to facilitator
1. At the start of this exercise participants may feel overburdened by the commitment to action. This exercise should help them realize that they can take action on various levels and in various ways. They gain a sense of support when they understand that they do not have to do something grandiose or take on a whole system in order to begin combating racism.
2. Sheet 2 lists action strategies that were developed by a group of students in a college dormitory. They can be adapted for other systems and institutions. Encourage the participants to adapt the list to fit their own setting.

Time 30 minutes

170

Commitment to Combat Racism

Sheet 1[1]

Indicate whether you have taken action on the items listed below. Check appropriate column.

Yes   No

_____ _____ 1. Have I aggressively sought out more information in an effort to enhance my own awareness and understanding of racism (talking with others, reading, listening)?

_____ _____ 2. Have I spent some time recently looking at my own racist attitudes and behavior as they contribute to or combat racism around me?

_____ _____ 3. Have I reevaluated my use of terms or phrases that may be perceived by others as degrading or hurtful?

_____ _____ 4. Have I openly disagreed with a racist comment, joke, or action among those around me?

_____ _____ 5. Have I made a personal contract with myself to take a positive stand, even at some possible risk, when the chance occurs?

_____ _____ 6. Have I become increasingly aware of racist TV programs, advertising, news broadcasts, etc? Have I complained to those in charge?

_____ _____ 7. Have I realized that White Americans are trapped by their own school, homes, media, government, etc., even when they choose not to be openly racists?

_____ _____ 8. Have I suggested and taken steps to implement discussions or workshops aimed at understanding racism with friends, colleagues, social clubs, or church groups?

_____ _____ 9. Have I been investigating political candidates at all levels in terms of their stance and activity against racist government practices?

[1]Developed by James Edler, University of Maryland.

_____ _____ 10. Have I investigated curricula of local schools in terms of their treatment of the issue of racism (also, textbooks, assemblies, faculty, staff, administration)?

_____ _____ 11. Have I contributed time and/or funds to an agency, fund, or program that actively confronts the problems of racism?

_____ _____ 12. Have my buying habits supported nonracist shops, companies, or personnel?

_____ _____ 13. Is my school or place of employment a target for my educational efforts in responding to racism?

_____ _____ 14. Have I become seriously dissatisfied with my own level of activity in combating racism?

Commitment to Combat Racism
Sheet 2

1. Educating roommates, close friends.
2. Raising issues in the dorm with heads of residence, resident directors, counseling staff, students, student government.
3. Providing information services—changing what normally appears on bulletin boards and walls to provocative posters, handouts, and other materials relevant to White racism.
4. Being a referral resource—directing Whites to people or groups who might be of assistance.
5. Acting as a race model, questioning the White power structure.
6. Establishing discussion groups, colloquia.
7. Finding films to expose White racism, developing new directions and strategies for Whites.
8. Finding out how dorm money is spent, using it to demonstrate meaningful concern about racism.
9. Working as a counselor with Whites who are genuinely interested in making sense of racial issues.

Exercise 44   The Costs and Benefits of Dealing
with Racism

Goals   1. To help participants explore their motives for becoming anti-
racist racists.
2. To help participants explore the price they pay for being racist
and/or becoming anti-racist racists.

Materials   Copies of "What Would I Give Up by Acting Against Racism?"
needed   (page 174)
Pens or pencils

Instructions 1. Hand out the sheet "What Would I Give Up by Acting Against
Racism?"
2. Ask the participants to fill out the sheet, being as honest as possible.
3. Discuss the responses and reactions.

Note to   1. This sheet focuses on participants' real motives for dealing with
facilitator   racism. It is especially important to spend time processing question
6, which highlights people's motives for becoming anti-racist
racists. It is also important to make sure that participants are
honest with themselves and the group about the prices they are
paying for being racists. Sometimes participants respond with the
answer they feel is "correct," rather than what they are really
feeling. Part of your responsibility in this exercise is to get to those
real feelings.
2. This exercise helps participants get in touch with the realities of
taking action steps so that they are clear about why they want to
do so. The facilitator must help them explore their motives and
reasons for wanting to take action. Some people may still be feeling
that they want to "help" Third World people. This is paternalistic
racism similar to the kind found in Exercise 37 ("After You, My
Dear Alphonse"). It is crucial that participants really understand
the assumption that racism is a White problem. It may be helpful

to ask them to fantasize the rewards they expect to gain from taking action. If they seem to expect thanks or gratitude from Third World people, they are engaging in paternalistic racism, similar to the kind reflected in Exercise 37 and in Exercise 40.

25 minutes   Time

What Would I Give Up by Acting Against Racism?

1. What would I give up by acting against racism?

2. How am I benefiting from racism?

3. What price am I paying for my racism?

4. What is my worst fantasy of what could happen if members of minorities were now in power?

5. What limits do I put on helping change institutional racism?

6. What needs of my own would I satisfy by being actively anti-racist?

Exercise 45   Dealing with Racism: Role Plays

1. To have participants develop alternative mechanisms and tools to Goals deal with racist situations.
2. To have participants try out in a role play some of these alternatives that they can use in their back-home situation.

Paper   **Materials**
Pens or pencils   **needed**

1. Ask participants to write down a racist situation that they have **Instructions** had to deal with. Have them explain on paper each person's position in the situation.
2. Collect and shuffle the papers. Ask for volunteers to role-play the situations.
3. Have group members do the role play. Process with the group and look at alternative actions.
4. Repeat the process.

This exercise is helpful in bringing participants into the framework **Note to** of their back-home situation. It is also helpful in giving them real **facilitator** and specific alternative actions that they can take.

10 to 15 minutes for each role play   **Time**

Exercise 46   Strategy and Action Planning

Goals
1. To help participants define and develop a specific action project to deal with their personal racism.
2. To help participants define and develop a specific action project to deal with racism in their environment.

Materials needed
Sheets from Exercises 42 and 43
Copies of Strategy and Action Plan (two per person) (page 180)

Instructions
1. Have the participants reread their sheets from Exercises 42 and 43.
2. Have them individually pick out at least one personal issue from Exercise 42 that they would like to explore further and, from Exercise 43, at least one action they can take to make changes in their environment.
3. Hand out two copies of the Strategy and Action Plan to each person. Ask the participants to fill out one copy for their personal objective and one for their institutional objective.
4. Have the participants share their projects. You may want to encourage people to work together on their institutional projects. This helps create a support system and encourages cooperation.
5. Ask the participants to list the next steps they must take to meet their objectives.
6. Have them share their next steps with the group. As part of this process ask them to share how they can help and support one another.

Note to facilitator
1. It is essential that participants be as clear as possible about their projects, as well as their course of action—that is, the next steps to take. Your role is to help participants clarify and be as specific as possible in developing their project forms.
2. It is also important to stress the need for a support system. The

178

members of the group must be able to identify their support system. Process this carefully when going over the Strategy and Action Plan.

3. It is important to point out to participants that whatever actions they take must not be taken in a vacuum—that is, they must be clear about whose needs they are trying to respond to. In a dormitory situation, for example, if a White student decides that his or her action project will be to seek the representation of Third World people on the house council, that student must discuss the action ahead of time with the Third World people in the dorm to see what their needs are. Perhaps the White student's action plan seeks only to get Third World representatives on the house council but without assuring them any power. The White person needs to check with the Third World community to see how his or her support can best be utilized. Again, Whites' efforts to "help" minorities are often forms of paternalism, not positive action. In dealing with *White* racism, action must be taken to deal with *White* people.

4. The facilitator should stress criteria for success and evaluation. One way to assess one's success is to set up a time line and try to get specific steps accomplished in a certain period. Sometimes suggesting that the group meet again in about a month to assess how well they have met their stated objectives is useful in helping them get started on taking some action.

5. Above all, remember that *inaction is racism.*

1 hour

Strategy and Action Plan

1. Identify the problem you want to resolve:

2. What are your *specific* goals?

3. What needs of your own will be fulfilled by achieving this goal?

4. What risks are involved? Are they worth it? (Yes, No)
   Risks:

5. What resources (people, support, materials) do you need to help achieve this goal?
   Resource:

   How Acquired:

6. What power and influence (formal and/or informal) do you have to reach this goal (include people who are important to the change effort)?

7. What resistance may you encounter? How can you decrease it?

8. What support do you have? How can you increase it?

9. What is the potential for success? What criteria will you use to evaluate your success?

10. What next steps must you take to meet this goal? Be specific.

Exercise 47   Evaluation and Feedback

1. To obtain feedback from participants on the facilitator's effective-ness. **Goals**
2. To obtain feedback and an evaluation of the strengths and weak-nesses of the workshop design.

Copies of FeedbackSheet (page 182) **Materials**
Pencils or pens **needed**

1. Hand out copies of the Feedback Sheet. **Instructions**
2. Ask the participants to fill it out as honestly and as specifically as possible.
3. Ask them to share with the group their feelings—positive or nega-tive—about the workshop itself and the role of the facilitator.

1. This sheet helps you gain a better idea of your strengths and weak-nesses. **Note to**
   facilitator
2. It is not necessary for the participants to share their comments with the group. Some participants do not want to disclose what they have written, and this preference should be accepted. Partici-pants will usually share with the group over-all general feelings. The more specific data come in the answers on the sheets.

20 minutes **Time**

Feedback Sheet: Course and Facilitator Evaluation

1. How helpful has this workshop been for you?

Not at all helpful					Somewhat helpful					Very helpful
0	1	2	3	4	5	6	7	8	9	10

2. List the ingredients (resources, exercises, and so on) that you feel were the most helpful to you. Why?

3. List the ingredients that you feel were the least helpful. Why?

4. Do you feel you have gained personally from this experience? If so, what did you gain? If not, what specific elements hindered you?

5. What changes would you recommend to improve this program?

6. How would you rate your facilitator?

Not effective					Somewhat effective					Highly effective
0	1	2	3	4	5	6	7	8	9	10

Why?

7. Additional comments:

Exercise 48   Closing

1. To bring the workshop to a close.   **Goals**
2. To leave participants thinking about their experience in the workshop as they say good-by.

Tape or record *War* (Selection "The World Is a Ghetto") (page 48)[1]   **Materials**
Record or cassette player   **needed**

1. It is time to end the workshop. One way to close is to use a media   **Instructions**
   selection that ties in some of the many issues with which the group
   has been struggling over the course of the workshop. A good selection is "War," listed above. It can be played as the final group
   experience.
2. An alternative is to use some experiential closing. A good resource
   for such exercises is J. William Pfeiffer and John E. Jones (eds.),
   Annual Handbook for Facilitators (yearly), (La Jolla, Calif.: University Associates).

Variable   **Time**

---

[1]Alternatives include Gil Scott Heron album *Winter in America* (selection "Peace Go
With You, Brother") or Dick Gregory album *Caught in the Act* (last selection, Gregory's farewell to nightclubs, stressing the importance of doing something for change,
as well as the power one person can have).

Appendix

READINGS AND RESOURCES

The Appendix lists resources and references that are useful in implementing this training program. Included are lists of readings for each stage of the training program for both facilitators and participants; sources of the films, tapes, records, forms, and other materials cited in the book; and a list of organizations that can provide additional materials and resources.

The materials listed below are suggestions. I encourage you to try to incorporate them in your program design. They serve as alternative perspectives that help clarify racism for the participants through various media—documents, song, dialogue, fiction, and so on. Some of the materials are presented through the eyes of Third World people; others are designed to show dimensions of racism that might not otherwise appear in the training sessions. Different people learn differently, and variety in experience will help make the program more meaningful to a greater number of participants.

My experience has been that structured and unstructured exercises, films, tapes, and readings help participants better understand the issues of racism on a number of levels. It is important that you adapt the program to fit your needs. Use the readings and resources appropriate to your setting, budget, time, and participants.

Readings

Readings play a vital role in supporting and developing the theories upon which this program is based.[1] They serve as one method of presenting new perspectives and data on White racism. Participants should be asked to read the materials before embarking on each stage. In that way they are better prepared for the experiences offered in the exercises. In addition, the readings add focus and meaning to each stage.

---

[1] An excellent extensive bibliography is National Institute of Mental Health, *Bibliography on Ethnicity and Ethnic Groups.* See Bibliography.

Most of the basic readings are handouts. Some of them are excerpts from books. The use of handouts in preference to books usually ensures that a wider range of resources and perspectives can be utilized.

The readings for each stage are divided into two sections:

1. Basic readings for participants and facilitator.
2. Supplementary readings, including books and articles for both participants and facilitators.

Clearly the lists are not exhaustive. They provide a foundation for each stage and sources for further exploration.

STAGE 1

Basic Readings

Anonymous. "White Racism: Definition and Types" (available through P.A.C.T., Detroit).

The most helpful part of this article is its discussion of racism in terms of types, including attitudinal and behavioral racism on individual and institutional levels. The article also presents specific examples and discussions of each type.

Bidol, P. *Racism Definition List.* Detroit: New Perspectives on Race, 1972 (available through P.A.C.T., Detroit).

This sheet was developed as a handy reference for definitions of prejudice, racism, and paternalistic racism.

Black News Service. "Third World Defined," *Collegian Newspaper* (University of Massachusetts), 1974.

A one-page article clarifying the term Third World.

Joyce, F. *An Analysis of American Racism* (pamphlet). Somerville, Mass.: New England Free Press, n.d. (available through P.A.C.T., Detroit).

Briefly discusses the history of racism and gives an in-depth definition of racism, explaining the kinds of racism and how they operate in American society. There are also sections on strategies and the need for action to combat racism.

Terry, R. "Racism Isn't Just . . ." (excerpt from a paper, "New Whites, Justice and Power"). Detroit: Detroit Industrial Mission, December 17, 1970, pp. 4–9 (available through P.A.C.T., Detroit).

Terry discusses the elements of racism and clearly differentiates racism from prejudice, bigotry, stereotyping, and discrimination to show that the terms should not be used interchangeably.

Viewpoint: Definition of Racism (pamphlet). New York: Council on Interracial Books, 1971.

This four-page pamphlet discusses various definitions of racism and prejudice and the kinds of racism—institutional, individual, and paternalistic.

Supplementary Readings

The following resources help clarify the concepts of Stage 1.

BOOKS AND PAMPHLETS

Allport, G. W. *The Nature of Prejudice.* New York: Doubleday, 1958.

One of the best resources on the elements of prejudice.

Bidol, P. *Mini-Lecture: Difference Between Prejudice and Racism* (pamphlet, available through P.A.C.T., Detroit).

Particularly useful to the facilitator not only in its clear discussion of the differences between prejudice and racism but also in the questions raised by the author. It presents a good overview of definitions, differences in terminology, and examples of how racism and prejudice operate in America today. The author emphasizes the meaning of racism for White people today. This lecture can be helpful in developing additional process questions for the exercises, or the facilitator may choose to read the entire lecture to the group.

Gossett, T. *Race: The History of an Idea in America.* New York: Schocken, 1963.

An excellent overview of the development of the concept of race. The author traces race theories from the ancient cultures of India and China to their manifestations in America from colonial days to the present.

Jones, J. *Prejudice and Racism.* Reading, Mass.: Addison-Wesley, 1972.

A comprehensive discussion of the elements of prejudice and racism and the way they operate in American society.

STAGE 2

The basic readings for Stage 2 present a general overview of institutional racism. The supplementary readings focus on specific aspects of institutional racism.

Basic Readings

Bennett, L., Jr. "White Problem in America," in *White Racism: Its History, Pathology, and Practice* (ed. by B. Schwartz and R. Disch). New York: Dell, 1970.

Discusses racism as a White problem. It looks at the "blaming the victim" syndrome and discusses basic ideologies contributing to inconsistencies between attitudes and behavior in White American society.

Institutional Racism in America: A Primer (pamphlet, available from Institutional Racism in America, Palo Alto, Calif.).

This pamphlet (an excerpt from L. Knowles and K. Prewitt, *Institutional Racism in America*), gives a brief general discussion of institutional racism. It looks at social policies, standards, control, justice, paternalism, caste, and class. It is essential for a basic understanding of institutional racism.

King, M. L., Jr. "I Have a Dream . . ." (speech delivered during march on Washington, 1963).

Discusses some of the issues in the liberation of Third World people, and focuses on the effects of racism. King highlights some of the goals for which civil rights activists are fighting.

Steinberg, D. *Definition and Analysis of White Racism* (pamphlet, available through P.A.C.T., Detroit).

Discusses White racism, including the issues of power and control. Also discusses how White racism functions in individual and institutional spheres.

Viewpoints (six pamphlets). New York: Council on Interracial Books, n.d.

Each four-page pamphlet discusses and describes a specific form of institutional racism, including media, police, jobs, housing, courts, and prisons.

Yette, S. "The Choice" and "The McCarran Act," in *The Choice.* New York: Putnam, 1971.

188

"The Choice," an excerpt from the Introduction of *The Choice,* briefly presents the issue of Black genocide in America as a result of White racism. "The McCarran Act," an excerpt from the text of *The Choice,* describes the act that provides the mechanism for establishing concentration camps in the United States. The two excerpts expose the cruel reality and the range of institutional racism in America.

Supplementary Readings

BOOKS

Bennett, J. L. *Before the Mayflower.* New York: Macmillan, 1966.

Brown, D. *Bury My Heart at Wounded Knee.* New York: Holt, Rinehart and Winston, 1970.

Fitzpatrick, J. *Puerto Rican Americans.* Englewood Cliffs, N.J.: Prentice-Hall, 1971.

Henderson, George, ed. *America's Other Children: Public Schools Outside Suburbia.* Norman: University of Oklahoma Press, 1971.

Josephy, A. *Red Power: The American Indian Fight for Freedom.* New York: McGraw-Hill, 1971.

Kitano, H. *Japanese Americans.* Englewood Cliffs, N.J.: Prentice-Hall, 1976.

Knowles, L., and K. Prewitt. *Institutional Racism in America.* Englewood Cliffs, N.J.: Prentice-Hall, 1969.

Myrdal, G. *An American Dilemma.* 2 vols. New York: Harper and Row, 1944.

Rogers, J. A. *World's Great Men of Color.* 2 vols. New York: Collier, 1946.

Ryan, W. *Blaming the Victim.* New York: Pantheon, 1971.

Schwartz, B., and R. Disch. *White Racism.* New York: Dell, 1970.

Steinfield, M. *Our Racist Presidents: From Washington to Nixon.* San Ramon, Calif.: Consensus, 1972.

Sue, S., and N. Wagner. *Asian Americans: Psychological Perspectives.* Palo Alto, Calif.: Science and Behavior, 1973.

Yette, S. *The Choice.* New York: Putnam, 1971.

ARTICLES AND PAMPHLETS

The materials listed below are grouped by topic.

Institutional Racism

Checklist on Racism. New York: Council on Interracial Books, n.d.
"Reverse Discrimination: Has It Gone Too Far?" *U.S. News and World Report,* March 29, 1975, pp. 26–29.
10 Quick Ways to Analyze Children's Books for Racism and Sexism. New York: Council on Interracial Books, n.d.
Welfare: Tell It Like It Is. Detroit: P.A.C.T., n.d.

Asian-Americans

Beck, K., and A. Beck. "All They Do Is Run Away," *Civil Rights Digest,* August, 1972.

Blacks

Hurst, C. "Malcolm X: The Meaning of His Life," *Chicago Tribune,* May 16, 1971.
Myths in Black History. Detroit: P.A.C.T., n.d.
Poussaint, A. "Cheap Thrills That Degrade Blacks," *Psychology Today,* Vol. 1, No. 9 (February, 1974), pp. 22, 26–27, 30, 32, 98.

Native Americans

Jackson, H. H. *A Century of Dishonor.* New York: Harper and Brothers, 1881, pp. 29–31, 336–42.
Nerhardt, J. "Butchering at Wounded Knee," in *Black Elk Speaks.* New York: Pocket Books, 1932, pp. 217–23.

STAGE 3

Basic Readings

This stage is process-oriented, and there are 'no basic readings. It is a time to focus on one's individual experiences. The readings suggested below are useful in helping White people sort through their racism, as well as serving as support.

Supplementary Readings

Berry, W. *The Hidden Wound.* Boston: Houghton Mifflin, 1970.

The author explores his own racism, including his hurts and pains. He discusses his fears of acknowledging his racism, as well as his desire to expose it. The more he discovers how deeply rooted his own racism is the more he wants to weed it out. He does so through accounts of personal experiences and analogies in literature.

Stalvey, L. *Education of a WASP.* New York: Morrow, 1970.

Lois Stalvey describes the development of her awareness of racism and the implications for her and her family. A very moving and personal account.

STAGE 4

Basic Readings

Burgest, D. "Racist Use of the English Language," *Black Scholar,* Vol. 4 (September, 1973), pp. 37–45.

This article presents a concise discussion of how language not only perpetuates racism but also hides it. The author gives many examples showing how the English language both contains and fosters a racist perspective. Included is a discussion of the cultural differences between Europeans and Africans. Reading this article is a necessary step in the exploration of cultural racism.

Forgan, H. *Teachers Don't Want to Be Labeled* (reprint of article). [Write to author for information on how to obtain this reprint.]

A one-page report of an experiment in which teachers' IQ's were measured and they were told that they scored lower than they actually did. The teachers experienced the anxiety caused by being labeled by "scores." The experiment helped them understand the effects of IQ testing on children's self-image.

Gibbs, J. T. "Black Students—White University: Different Expectations," *Personnel and Guidance Journal,* Vol. 51, No. 7 (1973), pp. 463–69.

Presents some of the problems Black students encounter as a result of the norms and culture of White universities. Discussed are the needs of Black students that the White system does not consider or respond to when it recruits Black students to enroll.

Other Side of Thanksgiving (reprint of article by Native Americans at University of Massachusetts, Amherst, Mass.). [Write to author for information on how to obtain this reprint.]

Discusses the inconsistencies between the celebration of Thanksgiving Day and the reality of the history of the White and Native American peoples. It is helpful for an understanding of the part cultural racism plays in the holidays Americans celebrate.

Supplementary Readings

BOOKS

Cleaver, E. *Soul on Ice.* New York: McGraw-Hill, 1968.
Cleaver presents, through essays and letters, a frank, strong picture of how Black identity develops. He helps the reader become aware of the effect of White racism on Blacks and discusses Black people's needs in American society.

Grier, W., and P. Cobbs. *Black Rage.* New York: Bantam Books, 1968.
Presents case after case showing the psychological effect of cultural racism on Black men and women.

—— and ——. *Jesus Bag.* New York: McGraw-Hill, 1971.
Explores the role of organized religion as an oppressive force against Blacks. Discusses how religion has perpetuated a sense of inferiority among Black people, while supporting and furthering a sense of superiority among White people.

Haley, A., ed. *Autobiography of Malcolm X.* New York: Grove Press, 1967.
Demonstrates what White racism does to a Black man from youth to adulthood. The agony Malcolm X endured from White racism is clearly expressed.

Jones, J. *Prejudice and Racism.* Reading, Mass.: Addison-Wesley, 1972.
Useful in the exploration of racism. The section on cultural racism is essential reading for the facilitator as well as for participants. It is extremely helpful in developing the mini-lecture on cultural racism, as well as serving as a guide for all the exercises in this stage.

Jordan, W. D. *White over Black: American Attitudes Toward the Negro, 1550–1812.* Baltimore: Penguin, 1968.
A guide to exploring and understanding Black people's attitudes, history, and culture.

ARTICLES

IQ

Billingsley, A., et al. "Perspectives on Inequality," *Harvard Educational Review,* Vol. 8 (1973).

Garcia, J. "The IQ Conspiracy," *Psychology Today,* Vol. 6, No. 4 (1972), pp. 40, 42–43, 90, 94.

Williams, R. "Scientific Racism and IQ: The Silent Mugging of the Black Community," *Psychology Today,* Vol. 7, No. 12 (1974), pp. 32, 34, 37, 38, 41, 101.

Winder, A. "Critique of Jensenism," *Massachusetts Review,* Vol. 11 (1970), pp. 812–22.

Racism and Sexism

Epstein, C. "Black and Female: The Double Whammy," *Psychology Today,* Vol. 7, No. 3 (1973), pp. 57–58, 60–61, 89.

"Feminism and Socialism," *Young Socialist,* Vol. 17, No. 3 (1973), pp. 9–12.

Lang, F. "The Mormon Empire," *Ramparts,* Vol. 10, No. 3 (1971), p. 40.

Olsen, M. "Cleanliness Is a Middle Class Racist Attitude," *"Education,"* Vol. 91, No. 3 (1971), pp. 274–76.

Porterfield, E. "Mixed Marriage," *Psychology Today,* Vol. 6, No. 8 (1973), pp. 71–72, 74–78.

"Racism/Sexism: Two Fronts, One War," *Detroit Industrial Mission,* Vol. 13, No. 5 (1972).

STAGE 5

Basic Readings

Bidol, P. *Reflections of Whiteness in a White Racist Society* (pamphlet). Detroit: P.A.C.T., n.d.

Specifically deals with the meaning of whiteness in America today. The author discusses the meaning of "White culture," the concept of "being White," and the responsibility for racism, as well as the psychological damage White people suffer from their racism.

Citron, A. *The Rightness of Whiteness: World of the White Child in a Segregated Society* (pamphlet). Detroit: Ohio Regional Educational Lab, 1969.

Looks at the effects of racism on White children. The author explores the elements that develop a White child's self-image and racist attitudes. He also highlights the ill-effects of racism on White children, showing how it causes internal conflict and confusion, and leaves them torn and culturally deprived. An excellent focus on White culture.

Supplementary Readings

BOOKS

Goodman, M. *Race Awareness in Young Children.* New York: Collier, 1964.

Describes studies of children's attitudes at different ages. Points out that children begin early to develop racist attitudes and knowledge of racial differences.

King, L. *Confessions of a White Racist.* New York: Viking, 1971.

King presents the process of his discovery of his own racism. He shares his perceptions of the luxuries afforded him because he is White, as well as the guilt he feels for all White racists. He also shares some of the struggles he has experienced trying to make sense out of the insanity of racism.

Kovel, J. *White Racism: A Psychohistory.* New York: Random House, 1971.

Describes White racist culture and institutions as products of America's White racist history. The author shows that racism is deeply ingrained in the psychology of White Americans.

ARTICLES

Kozol, J. "Where Have All the Flowers Gone? Racism in the Counter-Culture," *Ramparts,* 1972, pp. 30–32, 57.

A hard look at racism in free schools, which are shown to be a clear form of segregation. These schools are available to almost all White populations and are developed to meet White norms, needs, and values. The author discusses how the trends in the counter-culture perpetuate the same racism as those in the "straight" culture.

Welsing, F. *Cress Theory of Color Confrontation.* Washington, D.C.: Howard University, Department of Pediatrics, 1970.

Discusses the author's theory of the genetic inferiority of White people. Her arguments about why White people should explore their racism are very helpful for this stage. She presents some crucial data on the sociological and psychological effects of White racism on White people.

STAGE 6

Basic Readings

Barndt, J. "Setting the White Man Free," in *The White Problem.* New York: Presbyterian Distribution Service (225 Varick Street, New York, N.Y. 10014), 1970.

Highlights many of the issues discussed in all stages of this program. The author emphasizes the need to develop support and support systems in order to take action against racism.

Coppard, L., and B. Steinwachs. "Guidelines for Community Action," in *The White Problem.* New York: Presbyterian Distribution Service, 1970.

Presents a step-by-step process in taking action. It is extremely helpful in preparing participants for Stage 6, in which they follow a similar process.

Edler, J. *Distancing Behaviors* (pamphlet). Baltimore: University of Maryland, Department of Counseling, n.d.

Describes several games people play to avoid dealing with racism. These behaviors enable people to avoid taking action and serve as psychological "cop-outs." It is vital to understand and be aware of these traps.

Toward a Pluralistic Society (pamphlet). Reading, Mass.: Community Change, n.d.

A pamphlet presenting possible action strategies to combat racism. Designed for students, school administrators, teachers, superintendents, and school committees. Many of the strategies can be applied to other situations.

Vivian, C. T. *Death of Integration and a New Model* (pamphlet).

[Write to author for information on how to obtain this pamphlet.]

Presents the view that integration cannot work. White people have been in charge of integration. They did not want it to work, and so it is a dead issue. Interdependence is presented as a new model toward which Whites and minorities should be working. All groups need their independence, including their own power and control of institutions that serve their needs. They must be able to share and work together out of a desire to do so, not because of coercion.

Supplementary Readings

BOOKS

Terry, R. *For Whites Only.* Grand Rapids, Mich.: Eerdmans, 1970.
Discusses some possible answers and strategies to combat racism. Presents the concept of the "anti-racist racist." Gives direction and support to those who are trying to become anti-racist racists.

ARTICLES AND PAMPHLETS

Havrilesky, C. "Retooling the White Liberal," *Colloquy,* Vol. 3, No. 2 (1970).
A hard-hitting, satirical article emphasizing the effects of White people's efforts to "help" Blacks. Helps participants examine their rationales for their proposed action strategies.

New White Person (poster). Oakland, Calif.: Center for Social Change, n.d.
Describes some of the characteristics of the "New White Person." It is helpful in understanding the ultimate goal of this training program and the direction White people should be taking in liberating themselves from racism.

Taking the Next Steps. Cincinnati: United Methodist Church, Board of Missions, Women's Division (Service Center, 7820 Reading Road, Cincinnati, Ohio 45237), n.d.
A helpful booklet describing the issues of racism and mechanisms to develop action strategies. Presents additional insights that can be included in Stage 6.

Resources

Following is a list of materials suggested for use in the
program—films, tapes, records, simulations, instruments, and
pliers.

FILMS

Exercise	Film	Supplier
4	Black Thumb	King Screen Productions
		320 Aurora Avenue
		North Seattle, Wash. 98109
		or
		P.A.C.T. of Wayne County
		Community College
		163 Madison
		Detroit, Mich. 48226[1]
5	The Friendly Game	Mass Media Ministries
		2116 North Charles Street
		Baltimore, Md. 21218
		or
		P.A.C.T. (see above)
14	Black History: Lost,	Hampshire College
	Stolen, or Strayed	Audio Visual Department
	(Bill Cosby)	Amherst, Mass. 01002
		or
		P.A.C.T. (see above)
30	Ku Klux Klan	P.A.C.T. (see above)

TAPES OR RECORDS

Exercise	Tape or Record	Supplier
16	The Best of Buffy St. Marie	Available from most record stores
18	The Light Side: the Dark Side (Dick Gregory; Poppy Industries)	Available from most record stores

---

[1]Write to P.A.C.T. for a complete list of available materials. Examples are the films
On Prejudice (Bill Cosby), useful in Stage 1, and the series on Native Americans
(Marlon Brando), useful in Stage 2.

20	*Chastisement*	Available from most
	(Last Poets, Blue Thumb Record)	record stores
30	*Join the Klan*	Judy H. Katz
		Department of
		Human Relations
		University of Oklahoma
		Norman, Okla. 73019
33	*The Shockley-Poussaint Debate*	Radio Station WWRL
	(Spring, 1974)	New York, N.Y.
48	*War* ("The World Is a Ghetto")	Available from most
		record stores
48	*Winter in America*	Available from most
	(Gil Scott Heron; Strata	record stores
	East)	
48	*Caught in the Act*	Available from most
	(Dick Gregory)	record stores

MANUALS, FORMS

Exercise	*Manuals, Forms*	*Supplier*
11	Instruction manual for	Carole and Charles Camp
	Web of Institutional	71 Pond View Drive
	Racism	Amherst, Mass. 01002
21	Daniels Interracial Apper-	O. C. Bobby Daniels
	ception and Ideology Test	Associate Dean of Students
		University of Massachusetts
		Amherst, Mass. 01003
21	Black History Test	Coffin Associates
		21 Darling Street
		Marblehead, Mass. 01945
29	Brown, T. *Black Is . . .*	Grove Press, Inc.
		196 W. Houston Street
		New York, N.Y. 10014
29	Wilcox, P. *White Is . . .*	Grove Press, Inc.
		(see above)

ORGANIZATIONS

Many of the materials listed above are available from the following organizations, which can also provide additional resources on racism.

Center for Social Change
3137 Telegraph Avenue
Oakland, Calif.   94609

Community Change, Inc.
P.O. Box 146
Reading, Mass.   01867

Council on Interracial Books
CIBC Resource Center Room 300
1841 Broadway
New York, N.Y.   10023

Detroit Industrial Mission
13826 N. McNichols
Detroit, Mich.   38235

Institutional Racism in America
1140 Cowper Street
Palo Alto, Calif.   94301

Justice and Peace Center
3900 North Third Street
Milwaukee, Wisc.   53212

MARC
425 E. 15 K8
Bloomington, Ind.   47401

N.E. Free Press
60 Union Square
Somerville, Mass.   02143

P.A.C.T.
163 Madison
Detroit, Mich.   48226

Bibliography

Adams, P. *Attitude Exploration Survey*. Amherst, Mass.: University of Massachusetts, Center for Racial Understanding, 1973.

Allen, B. "Implications of Social Reaction Research for Racism," *Psychological Reports*, Vol. 29 (1971), pp. 883–91.

American Association of Colleges for Teacher Education, Commission on Multicultural Education. *No One Model American . . .* (pamphlet). Washington, D.C., 1972.

Authier, J. "A Step Group Therapy Program Based on Levels of Interpersonal Communication." Unpublished manuscript. Lincoln: University of Nebraska, College of Medicine, 1973.

———, K. Gustafson, B. Guerney, Jr., and J. Kasdorf. "The Psychological Practitioner as a Teacher: A Theoretical, Historical, and Practical Review," *Counseling Psychologist*, Vol. 5, No. 2 (1975), pp. 31–50.

Banks, J. *Teaching Strategies for Ethnic Studies*. Boston: Allyn and Bacon, 1975.

Barndt, J. "Setting the White Man Free," in *The White Problem* (ed. by E. L. Perry). Philadelphia: United Presbyterian Church, 1970, pp. 14–24.

Beck, J. *The Counselor and Black/White Relations*. Boston: Houghton-Mifflin, 1973.

Bennett, L. *Before the Mayflower: History of the Negro in America, 1619–1964*. New York: Macmillan, 1966.

Berry, W. *The Hidden Wound*. Boston: Houghton-Mifflin, 1970.

Bidol, P. *Reflections of Whiteness in a White Racist Society* (pamphlet). Detroit: P.A.C.T., 1971.

——— and R. C. Weber. *Developing New Perspectives on Race: An Innovative Multimedia Social Studies Curriculum in Race Relations for Secondary Level*. Detroit: New Detroit Speakers Bureau, 1970.

Breitman, G., ed. *By Any Means Necessary: Speeches, Interviews, and a Letter by Malcolm X*. New York: Pathfinder, 1970.

Brown, D. *Bury My Heart at Wounded Knee*. New York: Holt, Rinehart, 1970.

Brown, R. L. "Racism: Worst Tool of Cruelty," *Integrated Education*, Vol. 10 (1972), pp. 3–10.

Carmichael, S., and C. Hamilton. *Black Power: Politics of Liberation*. New York: Vintage, 1967.

Casselli, R. "Defining Racism," *Clearing House*, Vol. 46 (1971), pp. 98–101.

Citron, A. *The Rightness of Whiteness: World of the White Child in a Segregated Society* (pamphlet). Detroit: Ohio Regional Educational Lab, 1969 (available from P.A.C.T., Detroit).

Clark, K. *Prejudice and Your Child*. Boston: American, 1963.

Cleaver, E. *Soul on Ice*. New York: Dell, 1968.

Cobbs, P. "Ethnotherapy," *Intellectual Digest,* Vol. 2 (1972), pp. 26–28.

Comer, J. "White Racism: Its Root, Form, and Function," in *Black Psychology* (ed. by R. L. Jones). New York: Harper & Row, 1972.

Coppard, L. C., and B. J. Steinwachs. "Guidelines for Community Action," in *The White Problem* (ed. by E. L. Perry). Philadelphia: United Presbyterian Church, 1970.

Daniels, O. C. B. *Project RATE*. Amherst: University of Massachusetts, Student Affairs, 1974.

———. "The Relationship Between Interracial Apperception and Ideology." Ph.D. dissertation, University of Massachusetts, 1973.

Dekock, P. "Simulations and Changes in Racial Attitudes," *Social Education*, Vol. 33 (1969), pp. 181–83.

Delany, L. "The Other Bodies in the River," in *Black Psychology* (ed. by R. L. Jones). New York: Harper & Row, 1972.

Drum, D., and E. Knott. *Structured Groups for Facilitating Development*. New York: Human Sciences, 1977.

Du Bois, W. E. B. *Darkwater*. New York: Harcourt, Brace & Howe, 1920.

———. *Souls of Black Folk*, in *Three Negro Classics* (ed. by John H. Franklin). New York: Avon, 1965 (originally published in 1903).

Edler, J. "White on White: An Anti-Racism Manual for White Educators in the Process of Becoming." Ed.D. dissertation, University of Massachusetts, 1974.

Fanon, F. *The Wretched of the Earth*. New York: Grove, 1968.

Gay, G. "Organizing and Designing a Culturally Pluralistic Curriculum," *Educational Leadership*, Vol. 52 (1973), pp. 176–79, 181–83.

Goldin, P. "Model for Racial Awareness Training for Teachers in Integrated Schools," *Integrated Education*, Vol. 8 (1970), pp. 62–64.

Goodman, M. E. *Race Awareness in Young Children*. New York: Collier, 1964.

Greenwald, H. J., and D. B. Oppenheim. "Reported Magnitude of Self Misidentification Among Negro Children," *Journal of Social Psychology*, Vol. 8 (1968), pp. 49–52.

Grief, W., and P. Cobbs. *Black Rage*. New York: Bantam, 1968.

Haley, A., ed. *Autobiography of Malcolm X*. New York: Grove, 1967.

Hanson, P., P. Rothous, W. O'Connell, and G. Wiggins. "Training

Patients for Effective Participation in Back Home Groups," *American Journal of Psychiatry*, Vol. 126 (1969), pp. 857–62.

Hunt, G., and N. A. Azrin. "A Community-Reinforcement Approach to Alcoholism," *Behavior Research and Therapy,* Vol. 11 (1973), pp. 91–104.

Hunter, J. "Teaching to Eliminate Black-White Racism: An Educational Systems Approach," *Journal of Geography*, Vol. 71 (1972), pp. 87–95.

Ivey, A. "The Counselor as Teacher," *Personnel and Guidance Journal*, Vol. 54, No. 8 (1976), pp. 431–33.

———. *Microcounseling: Innovations in Interviewing Training.* Springfield, Ill.: C. C. Thomas, 1971.

Johnson, J. W. *Autobiography of an Ex-Colored Man.* New York: Hill and Wang, 1960.

Jones, J. *Prejudice and Racism.* Reading, Mass.: Addison-Wesley, 1972.

Jordan, W. *White over Black: American Attitudes Toward the Negro, 1550–1812.* Baltimore: Penguin, 1968.

Joyce, Frank. *An Analysis of American Racism* (pamphlet). Boston: N.E. Free Press, n.d.

Katz, J., and A. Ivey. "Developing the Counselor as Teacher: A Systematic Program," *Canadian Counselor,* in press.

——— and ———. "White Awareness: The Frontier of Racism Awareness Training," *Personnel and Guidance Journal,* Vol. 55, No. 8 (1977), pp. 485–89.

Kerner Commission. *National Advisory Commission on Civil Rights.* New York: Bantam, 1968.

Knowles, L., and K. Prewitt, eds. *Institutional Racism in America.* Englewood Cliffs, N.J.: Prentice-Hall, 1969.

Kovel, J. *White Racism: A Psychohistory.* New York: Pantheon, 1970.

Kranz, P. L. "Racial Confrontation Group Implemented Within a Junior College," *Negro Educational Review*, Vol. 23 (1972), pp. 70–80.

Lacy, D. *White Use of Blacks.* New York: McGraw-Hill, 1972.

Marrow, A. J. "Events Leading to the Establishment of the National Training Laboratories," *Journal of Applied Behavioral Science,* Vol. 3 (1967), pp. 144–50.

Maultsby, M. "The ABC's of Solving Your Own Emotional Problems." Unpublished paper, 1970.

Moore, R. "A Rationale, Description, and Analysis of a Racism Awareness Program for White Teachers." Ed. D. dissertation, University of Massachusetts, 1973.

Morland, J. "Racial Acceptance and Preference of Nursery School Children in a Southern City," *Merrill-Palmer Quarterly*, Vol. 8 (1962), pp. 372–80.

Myrdal, G. *An American Dilemma.* 2 vols. New York: Harper & Row,

1944.

National Institute of Mental Health. *Bibliography on Ethnicity and Ethnic Groups.* Rockville, Md.: U.S. Department of Health, Education and Welfare, n.d.

Pierce, R., and J. Drasgow. "Teaching Facilitative Interpersonal Functioning to Psychiatric Patients," *Journal of Counseling Psychology,* Vol. 16 (1969), pp. 295–98.

Quarles, B. *The Negro in the Making of America.* New York: Collier, 1964.

Rathus, S. "Instigation of Assertive Behavior Through Videotape-mediated Assertive Models and Direct Practice," *Behavior Research and Therapy,* Vol. 11 (1973), pp. 57–65.

Roberts, D. "The Treatment of Cultural Scripts," *Transactional Analysis Journal,* Vol. 5, No. 1 (1975), pp. 29, 31, 35.

Robinson, R., and E. Spaights. "Study of Attitudinal Change Through Lecture Discussion Workshop," *Adult Education,* Vol. 19 (1969), pp. 163–71.

Rubin, I. "The Reduction of Prejudice Through Laboratory Training," *Journal of Applied Behavioral Science,* Vol. 3 (1967), pp. 29–51.

Ryan, W. *Blaming the Victim.* New York: Random House, 1971.

Schwartz, B., and R. Disch, eds. *White Racism: Its History, Pathology, and Practice.* New York: Dell, 1970.

Singh, J., and A. Yancey. "Racial Attitudes in White First Grade Children," *Journal of Educational Research,* Vol. 67 (1974), pp. 370–72.

Steckler, G. "Authoritarian Ideology in Negro College Students," *Journal of Abnormal Social Psychology,* Vol. 54 (1957), pp. 396–99.

Steinberg, D. *Racism in America: Definition and Analysis* (pamphlet, available through P.A.C.T., Detroit), n.d.

Synnestvedt, S. "White Faces and White Studies," *Commonweal,* Vol. 92 (1970), pp. 182–83.

Terry, R. *For Whites Only.* Grand Rapids, Mich.: Eerdmans, 1970.

Thomas, A., and S. Sillen. *Racism and Psychiatry.* New York: Brunner-Mazel, 1972.

Timmel, S. *White on White Handbook.* Cambridge, Mass.: Robinson and Richardson, n.d.

Uhlemann, M. "Behavioral Change Outcomes and Marathon Group Therapy." Master's thesis, Colorado State University, 1968.

U.S. Commission on Civil Rights. *Racism in America and How to Combat It.* Washington, D.C.: U.S. Government Printing Office, 1970.

U.S. Commission on Mental Health. *Joint Commission on Mental Health.* Washington, D.C.: U.S. Government Printing Office, 1965.

Walker, J., and L. Hamilton. "A Chicano/Black/White Encounter," *Personnel and Guidance Journal,* Vol. 51 (1973), pp. 471–77.

Welsing, F. C. "Conspiracy to Make Blacks Inferior," *Ebony*, Vol. 29 (1974), pp. 84–94.

———. *Cress Theory of Color Confrontation*. Washington, D.C.: Howard University, 1972.

Wilkinson, C. B. "Problems in Black-White Encounter Groups," *International Journal of Group Psychotherapy*, Vol. 23 (1973), pp. 155–65.

Winter, S. K. "Black Man's Bluff," *Psychology Today*, Vol. 5 (1971), pp. 39–43, 78–81.

Yette, S. *The Choice*. New York: Putnam, 1971.

Young, W. "Exceptional Children: Text of a Keynote Speech." Reston, Va.: Council for Exceptional Children, 1970.

Index

Adams, P.: 30
Affirmative Action programs: 5, 7, 78
Allen, B.: 12–13
American Association of Colleges for Teacher Education: 18
American dilemma: *see* racism
Anglo-Saxons: 14–15
Asian-Americans: 4, 136, 142
Assertiveness training: 20
Attitude Exploration Survey: 30
Authier, J.: 20–21
Azrin, N. A.: 20

Banks, J.: 18
Barndt, Joseph R.: 10, 14
Basic communications-skills program: 20
Beck, J.: 11, 13–14
Behavioral Rating Scale: 30
Bennett, L.: 8, 15
Berry, W.: 11
Bias: 33
Bidol, P.: 12–13, 17, 18, 19, 41
Bigotry: 33
Black (color): 8, 57, 110, 113–18; negative connotation of, 13; and language, 113–16
Black History Week: 69
Black Power: 7
Blacks: 4, 15, 17, 136–37, 140, 142, 146; effects of racism on, 7; perspective of, on racism, 80; and being Black, 107; myths about, 109
Breitman, G.: 16, 18
Brown, D.: 10, 12

Brown Power: 7
Busing: 7, 78

Carmichael, Stokely: 16, 29
Casselli, R.: 11
Caucasians: *see* Whites
Change agents: 5
Chicanos: 4, 17, 137, 142
Children: racial attitudes of, 13–14; and pluralistic society ideals, 18
Citron, A.: 11–15
Civil rights: 4, 80
Clark, Kenneth: 12
Cleaver, E.: 15, 19
Cobbs, F.: 10, 11, 16
Cognitive approach to racism: 17–18
Comer, J.: 12
Commission on Civil Rights, U.S.: 16
Commission on Mental Health, U.S.: 11
Community-Reinforcement Alcohol Treatment Program: 20
Coppard, L. C.: 16
Cosby, Bill: 73
Counselors: 5, 65, 67

Daniels, O. C. B.: 14
Dekock, P.: 17
Delaney, L.: 12
Disch, R.: 8–9, 13
Drum, D.: 20
DuBois, W. E. B.: 7, 11, 13

Edler, J.: 15, 17, 19
Education: racism in, 5, 16, 55, 63–71, 77; English language in,

113–14
Educators: 5
Ellis' Rational Emotive Therapy: 20
Employment, racism in: 5, 85
Encounter groups: 16, 22; inter-
  racial, 17

Facilitators: 5, 25–27, 30
Fanon, F.: 10
Feedback: 20, 111, 169, 181–82

Gay, G.: 18
Genocide: 10, 77
Ghettos: 4, 7, 9; white, 15
Golden, P.: 17
Goodman, M. E.: 13
Greenwald, H. J.: 13
Gregory, Dick: 80, 118
Grier, W.: 10
Guerney, B., Jr.: 20–21
Gustafson, K.: 20–21

Haley, A.: 9–10
Hamilton, C.: 16
Hamilton, L.: 16–17
Hanson, P.: 20
History, white: 19, 69, 74, 89
Housing, racism in: 55
Human relations: scope of, 3; prob-
  lems of, 3–4; and racism, 3–6, 16,
  19–20
Human Relations Training Pro-
  gram, Houston Veterans Admin-
  istration Hospital, 20
Hunt, G.: 20
Hunter, John M.: 18

Identity, racial: 4
Integration: 7, 78
IQ tests: 69, 80, 90, 124–32; and
  Shockley-Poussaint debate, 133
Ivey, A.: 5, 20, 26

Jackson, Shirley: 146

Japanese-Americans: 4
John Birch Society: 7, 120
Johnson, James Weldon: 14–15
Joint Negro College Fund: 87
Jones, J.: 9, 11, 122–23
Jones, John E.: 183
Jordan, W.: 8, 12
Joyce, Frank: 8

Kasdorf, J.: 20–21
Katz, J.: 5, 20, 26
Kerner Commission: 7; report of,
  9–10
King, Martin Luther, Jr.: 69
Knott, E.: 20
Knowles, L.: 9, 14–15
Kovel, J.: 8–9, 11–12
Kranz, P. L.: 16–17
Ku Klux Klan: 7, 119–20

Lacy, D.: 8, 10
Language, racism in: 5, 113–18
Last Poets, the: 89, 118

Malcolm X: 16, 18, 69
Manifest destiny, doctrine of: 4, 60,
  77
Marrow, A. J.: 16
Maultsby, M.: 20
Minorities: 4, 8, 10–11, 14, 17, 19,
  109, 143; see also Third World
  Americans
Moore, R.: 19
Morland, J.: 13
Multicultural curricula: 18; short-
  comings of, 19
Myrdal, Gunnar: 7, 12, 34

NAACP Legal Defense Fund: 87
Native Americans: 4, 8–9, 69, 116,
  137, 142
Negroes: see Blacks
North (U.S.): 4, 7

208

O'Connell, W.: 20
Oppenheim, D. B.: 13

Pfeiffer, J. William: 183
Pierce, R., and Drasgow, J.: 20
Politics, racism in: 55
Prejudice: 33, 40–45
Prewitt, K.: 9, 14–15
Psychotherapy: 20

Quarles, B.: 13

Race-relations history: 17–18
Racism: 3, 17, 19, 53, 81, 110;
    extent of, 4–6, 9; as White prob-
    lem, 6–30, 78, 167; effects of, 7,
    10–15; inaction about, 10, 19,
    95, 167, 179; and genocide, 10;
    as disease, 11–12, 25; as form of
    schizophrenia, 11, 15; and mech-
    anisms for change, 15–21; defi-
    nitions of and inconsistencies in,
    33–36, 47–50, 53, 59, 76, 114,
    161, 164–65, 169; institutional,
    53–90; kinds of, 55–57, 93; levels
    of, 56–57; cultural, 109–32; per-
    sonal, 109, 161–62; and Ku Klux
    Klan, 119–20; paternalistic, 147,
    174, 179; development of action
    on, 169; and combat commitment,
    170–73; see also white racism
Rathus, S.: 20
Red Power: 7
Reservations, Indian: 4
Reverse discrimination: see reverse
    racism
Reverse racism: 7, 35, 54
Roberts, D.: 4
Robinson, R.: 13
Rothous, P.: 20
Rubin, I.: 16–17

Schwartz, B.: 8–9, 13
Sillen, S.: 12

Simulation game: 17
Singh, J.: 13
Slavery: 4, 9, 89
South (U.S.): 4, 7
Spaights, E.: 13
Steckler, G.: 30
Steckler Anti-Black and Anti-White
    scales: 30
Steinberg, D.: 19
Steinwachs, B. J.: 16
Synnestvedt, S.: 17
Systematic Step Group Therapy
    Program: 20

Terry, R.: 9, 16–17, 19
T-groups: 16–17, 34
Third World Americans: 4, 9–10,
    14–15, 17, 24, 35, 47, 49, 53–54,
    61–65, 69, 75, 90, 93, 100, 109,
    111, 113, 117, 136, 140, 174–75;
    see also minorities
Thomas, A.: 12
Timmel, S.: 19

Uhlemann, M.: 20, 22, 30
Urban League: 87

Violence: 17, 62

Walker, J.: 16–17
Weber, R. C.: 18
Welsing, Francis Cress: 7, 9, 12, 15
White-awareness training: see
    White-on-White workshop
White-on-White workshop: 19; ob-
    jectives and goals, 22–23; assump-
    tions of, 23–24; content and pro-
    cess, 25–26; facilitator in, 5,
    25–27, 30; stages of, 26, 28–29;
    exercises, 26, 28; groups, 27;
    flexibility, adaptability of, 27–28;
    formats, 28–29; measuring effec-
    tiveness of, 29–30; see also work-
    shop (stages)

White racism: 21; historical, 4; and racial myths, 5; effects of, 9–15; and ideologies, 12, 34–35, 60, 80, 110; and strategies for change, 15–21; institutional, 53, 55–61, 63–90; power of, 61, 100; cultural, 109–32; personal, 109, 161–62; *see also* racism

Whites: 4, 17, 136–37, 140, 142, 144–46; discrepancies of, 5, 8; and racial myths, 5, 98–99, 109, 155; attitudes of, 5, 80, 93, 134–35, 169; behaviors of, 5, 164–65, 169; training programs for, 5–6, 22–31; effects of racism on, 7, 10–15; and superiority attitudes, 7, 12–13; oppression by, 9; and history, 19; reeducation of, 93; guilt feelings of, 93–95, 137, 144; fears of, 98–99; feelings of power of, 100–101; and being white, 106–107

Wiggins, G.: 20

Wilkinson, C. B.: 16

Winter, S. K.: 16

Women's Movement: 4, 24, 27

Workshop, Stage 1: objectives and goals of, 33–34, 37–38, 40, 43–44, 46, 48–51; method of, 34–36; and facilitator, 37–38, 41, 47; concentric-circles exercise in, 38–39; definition of prejudice in, 40–42, 50; Prejudice Definition Sheet in, 40–41; "Mini-Lecture on the Difference Between Prejudice and Racism" in, 41; and *Black Thumb* (film), 43; and *The Friendly Game* (film), 44–45; design for racist community in, 46–48; "Racism Is . . ." sheet in, 46–47; fuzzy concept exercise in, 48; definition of racism in, 49–51; Racism Definition Sheet in, 49

————, Stage 2: rationale of, 53–54; method of, 54; "Mini-Lecture: Kinds and Levels of Racism" in, 55–58; goals of, 55, 59, 61, 63, 70, 73, 75, 77, 80, 82, 89; and facilitator, 57–59, 61–63, 71, 73, 76–77, 79, 81–82, 89; "Racism Is . . ." sheet in, 58; and inconsistencies, 59; and ideologies and slogans, 60; simulation game in, 61–62; simulation experience in, 63–64; Simulation Design 1: College Setting in, 65–66; Simulation Design 2: Public School Setting in, 67–69; and "The Drawbridge" (story), 70–72; and *Black History: Lost, Stolen, or Strayed* (film), 73–74; and power of institutional racism, 75–76; and institutional racism and Native Americans, 77; and *The Best of Buffy St. Marie* (record), 77; and institutional-racism debate, 78–79; and institutional racism, 80–81, 83–90; and *The Light Side: The Dark Side* (record), 80; and racism in institutions, 82; "Inventory of Racism" in, 82; and white American history, 89; and *Chastisement* (The Last Poets, recording), 89; and Daniels Interracial Appreciation and Ideology Test, 90; and Black History Test, 90

————, Stage 3: rationale of, 93–94; method of, 94–95; objectives and goals of, 97–98, 100, 102, 105; and facilitator, 97–98, 101–102, 105; Here-and-Now Wheel Exercise in, 97; and fears about racism, 98–99; and White power, 100; and feelings of exclusion, 100–101; Circle Break-in Exercise in, 100–101; and fears and fantasies, 102–104; "Fantasy: Bus

210

Trip" in, 102–103; "Whose Fantasy?" in, 102, 104; "Inventory of Racial Experience" in, 105; and personal experiences, 105–107

———, Stage 4: and cultural racism, 109; and personal racism, 109; rationale of, 107–11; and language and racism, 113–16; objectives and goals of, 113, 115, 117, 119, 121, 133; and facilitator, 113, 116, 123, 133; "Black Is. . ." in, 117–18; "White Is . . ." in, 117–18; and *Join the Klan* (tape), 119; and *Ku Klux Klan* (film), 119; and historical roots of cultural racism, 121–23; Dove Counter Balance Test in, 124–32; and Shockley-Poussaint debate, 133

———, Stage 5: and personal attitudes and behavior, 135–47; rationale of, 135–36; method of, 136–37; objectives and goals of, 139, 142, 152, 155, 161; and facilitator, 137, 140, 142–43, 152, 155; personal checklist of, 141; "Being White in America Today is like . . ." in, 142–43 & n.; "White Is Beautiful" (slogan) in, 144–45; self-image study in, 146–47; and "After You, My Dear Alphonse" (story), 148–51; Values Clarification Exercise in, 152–54; and racist attitudes, 155; "Thirty Statements" (test) in, 155–60; owning of whiteness in, 161–62; "A Vision of Equality" in, 161–63; and inconsistencies, 164–65

———, Stage 6: objectives and goals of, 167–68, 178, 181, 183; anti-racist racist defined in, 167; and costs and benefits of action, 167–68, 174–76; method of, 168; "Discovering Inconsistencies Between Attitude and Behavior" in, 169; "Actions I Can Take" in, 169; and facilitator, 169, 174, 177; "Commitment to Combat Racism" in, 170–73; role plays in, 177; strategy and action planning in, 178–80; evaluation and feedback in, 181–82; and workshop close, 183; and *The World Is a Ghetto* (record), 183 & n.; and *Annual Handbook for Facilitators,* 183

World War II: 9

Yancy, A.: 13
Yellow Power: 7
Yette, S.: 9–10
Young, Whitney: 9